The Ohio Guide to Firearm Laws

Fifth Edition

BY

KEN HANSON, ATTORNEY AT LAW

ORPA & NRA LIFE MEMBER, NRA CERTIFIED INSTRUCTOR AND RANGE SAFETY OFFICER

KHANSON@FBYLAW.COM

740-363-1213

PAGE LAYOUT AND COVER DESIGN BY JUSTIN SCHAEFER/PHOTOTEXT

TABLE OF CONTENTS

PREFACE

Thanks to Alan Korwin at Bloomfield Press who originally suggested that I write this book.

Thanks to the tireless members and volunteers across the state who work for firearm rights. Whether it is writing a letter to the editor, a phone call to your politician or volunteering your time with youth shooting/hunting activities, if you were not doing it, no one would be.

Thanks to Professors Bob Krivoshey and Lou Jacobs at the OSU College of Law. Despite being hopeless liberals, they are wonderful human beings who were eager to take this clueless federalist/libertarian under their wings and show that criminal prosecution work is the noblest way to go broke while practicing law.

Thanks to Professor Lawrence Herman at OSU's Moritz College of Law. Through about 1500 pages of hand-selected materials, photocopied and spiral-bound, he developed a wonderfully advanced yet attainable Police Procedures and Evidence Gathering class that enabled me to gain more practical, applicable knowledge than in any other class in law school. I still, to this day, keep his class materials in my office.

Thanks to all of my friends in various governmental positions who help out the cause in subtle ways. If I mentioned you by name, you would probably get in trouble. You know who you are. I have decided it is safe to start sharing some of the stories of how a bill becomes a law, but I still won't name names, unless it is safe for them for me to do so.

Thanks to my family for their patience, love and support. More times than I want to admit, on a weekend or weeknight, they've watched me drive off to a concealed carry class, an informational presentation, or increasingly rarely, due to my teaching schedule, off to the range. Although I enjoy what I do immensely, in many ways I do it for them. It is important to me that my son and daughter have the choice to live as free citizens, and maybe 15 years from now, they'll look back and think "wow, Dad was part of that." The tattoo was all for me, though, and my wife was gracious enough not to kill me over it. Hopefully my daughter, Miranda Arizona Hanson, will understand when she finally discovers what her namesake is all about.

I have been giving presentations to concealed carry classes on Ohio's firearm laws since December 2003, averaging at least 4 classes per month. I also teach Continuing Legal Education for attorneys. This book goes into far more detail than my class presentations and approaches the level of detail I go into in my CLE classes for attorneys. By design, I limit these materials to the information most directly relevant to the majority of gun owners, and leave the more esoteric portions of the law untouched. Since a significant portion of these people also say they like to carry copies of the applicable laws with them in the car, at work etc., this book continues to provide digested copies of all relevant firearm statutes in their current form, all in one place.

Please do me one favor: If you are trying to educate a police officer or politician on the law, do not waive this book in his or her face and scream about how you "know your rights." You aren't helping gun rights in Ohio with this confrontational behavior. Polite conversations work much better.

This book is not intended to be an exhaustive treatise on firearm laws. It is intended to be an outline of firearm laws applicable to a citizen who is interested in obtaining a concealed carry license and complying with the law. Certain exceptions can and do exist to the materials presented in this book, and competent legal counsel should be sought by individuals desiring specific legal advice addressing their particular circumstances.

This information is general and educational in nature. It does not constitute legal advice, and no attorney client relationship is intended or assumed. In an effort to be more user friendly and understandable to a layperson, these materials will often make a generalized summary rather than reciting language from the applicable sections of the law word by word. The statutes in their word-by-word form are presented in Appendix A.

The application of laws is a peculiar, fact-specific and sometimes irrational process. In most instances, there is no way to give a guaranteed, black-letter law answer that will apply to every possible variation. It is the intention of this book to provide the highest level of information possible while still being accessible to the layperson.

As a matter of general policy, this book does not cover the specific levels of penalties involved for violating any of these laws. Ambitious prosecutors can, and do, find many different ways to criminally charge one set of actions. It simply is not possible, to a degree of certainty, to say that if you do x, y, and z then it will only be a second degree misdemeanor. There is no such thing as a "good crime." If something is illegal, then the average, law-abiding gun owner is not going to do it, regardless of what degree of offense the conduct involves. Beyond stating the obvious "crime=bad", I can easily show you one set fact pattern, and then explain how that conduct could be charged as a 4th degree misdemeanor OR as a 1st degree misdemeanor OR as a 3rd degree felony OR as a 2nd degree felony. It all depends upon how ornery your prosecutor is feeling.

There is a tremendous amount of bad information on Ohio Concealed Carry in circulation, coming from any number of "authoritative" sources. Part of the problem is that there is a shortage of attorneys who have made the investment needed to become thoroughly familiar with this subject matter. Part of the problem is that any number of persons are giving what amounts to legal advice, without being qualified to do so, and without knowing the Golden Rule of Lawyers: "Know when to say I don't know." Even in 2015, I continue to receive reports from people who have attended presentations for "self-defense legal plans" established by attorneys, and the attorney is giving the audience incorrect statements of Ohio Law. The final part of the problem is that the law is very complex, and by its very nature, is difficult to understand, and even more difficult to summarize and convey to others.

When evaluating a source of information, the gun owner should look to see whether the source has made the actual investment to learn the subject matter, is able to communicate the majority of the subject matter in an understandable manner, and is willing to occasionally be stumped by a question and go back to the books and find the answer, rather than guessing to save face. Has the person tried self-defense cases in court? Have they been successful? Is this something this person has done for many years, or did they just start in the last few years on a whim? Personally, I find myself researching new questions, or double-checking myself, at least once per month.

This book is now a Fifth Edition, which follows a 4.5 prior Editions (there was a CD ROM update to the second edition). It is always good practice to review what you think you know. While the Fifth Edition contains material that was in the prior Editions, the Fifth Edition also contains much new material and updated statutes/legal analysis.

I am often asked during my presentations why things in Ohio are messed up the way they are. The readers' feedback shows there is a demand and interest in editorial commentary and analysis versus formal writing style, so as with prior Editions, I will continue to use much more first-person writing and opinion than the last editions, and will tell "behind the scenes" stories of the legislative battles of the past 11+ years. I hope pure non-fiction readers/editors out there excuse the license I have taken in abandoning a purer, objective approach.

I am going to to refer to myself in the first person "I" and the reader in the second person "you" whenever possible, rather than using the sanctimonious "this author" and/or "the reader," "the gun owner" etc. I can spend time hunting and killing every last grammar, spelling and stylistic mistake, wearing out a copy of the AP Stylebook while juggling Strunk and White, or I can spend time working for your gun rights. Since I am the only one with a vote, we're going with less formal writing. Similarly, I learned to type with non-scalable fonts, so I double space after the period at the end of a sentence. I could spend time trying to force-break this habit, proofreading to make sure I only single spaced, or I can spend my time elsewhere.

As a final note, as you begin to read about the legislative battles, please always keep in mind two things. First, self-defense knows no ideological bounds. The mere fact that some person has an (R) or a (D) after their name does not tell you anything about that person's commitment to your right to defend yourself and family. I can state with a clean conscience that there are members of both major political parties who oppose your rights, and members of both major parties who support your rights. Do everyone a favor, before you push that button in the voting booth, make sure that you have examined that person's record on guns. You WILL be surprised.

Second, much of what is accomplished to advance your gun rights comes back to volunteer involvement. A law is passed because of phone calls, emails and letters to your elected officials, or volunteers working on the campaign of a pro-gun legislator facing an anti-gun opponent. That law then gets applied statewide in various courts and in various jurisdictions, and the result is that people in all 88 counties have benefited from you volunteering five minutes to make that legislative contact or one afternoon to go hand out literature for that candidate. Similarly, rogue judges who refuse to follow the rule of law are thwarted on appeal because your voluntary donation paid for court costs or attorney fees, and now that judge is exposed as a renegade and volunteers can work for that judge's opponent in a race that offers a clear choice between an anti-gun candidate and a (hopefully) pro-gun candidate. I can't stress this enough. Your five minutes or your $20 donation makes all the difference in the world.

Ohio is a code law state, meaning Ohio does not have common-law criminal offenses. In order for conduct to be criminal, the conduct must be prohibited by some section of the Ohio Revised Code (R.C.) Unfortunately, there are several linear yards of shelf space taken up by the Ohio Revised Code.

For the most part, when something is referred to as "criminal", what is meant is that the conduct is prohibited someplace within Title 29 of the Ohio Revised Code. However, criminal charges are contained throughout the Revised Code.

Most traffic offenses generally are not considered criminal, and most of these traffic offenses are set forth in Title 45 of the Revised Code. Ohio's body of criminal law can be categorized broadly in two categories: misdemeanor and felony.

Felony offenses are the most severe, punishable by higher fines, actual time in prison (compared to county jail for misdemeanors) and loss of civil rights. Those convicted of a felony punishable by more than 12 months in prison (in Ohio a fourth degree felony or higher) are under federal firearm disability and cannot own or posses firearms. As will be discussed in Chapter 2, the Ohio gun owner needs to be aware that not just felony convictions will disqualify a citizen from owning a firearm and/or getting a concealed carry license. Some misdemeanors and some fifth degree felonies (which are punishable by 12 months or less) also disqualify a citizen from owning a firearm.

Misdemeanors, or petty offenses, are punishable by fines and county jail time. The total possible penalty exposure for misdemeanors is lower than for felonies, and misdemeanors typically do not disqualify a citizen from firearm ownership. By way of illustration, the following chart (taken from the LSC summary of H.B. 86 effective September 27, 2011) illustrates the typical punishment ranges and the differences in penalties:

Category	Jail Time		Prison Time
F1	Possible		3-11 Years
F2	Possible		2-8 Years
F3	Possible		0.66-5 Years
F4	Possible		6-18 Months
F5	Possible		6-12 Months
M1	Up to 6 Months		No
M2	Up to 90 Days		No
M3	Up to 60 Days		No
M4	Up to 30 Days		No
MM	No		No

In addition, if a person uses a firearm to commit a felony, a gun specification can be added to the charge. A gun specification is simply an "add-on" to an underlying criminal charge, an addition to the indictment where the grand jury adds to the underlying offense by specifying the offender possessed a firearm while committing the offense. A firearm specification, if proven, adds mandatory prison time of varying lengths to any other penalty or sentence imposed by the Court for the underlying charge.

The gun owner in Ohio needs to be very aware of firearm specifications existing within our laws. No one is against indicting a home invader wielding a gun for burglary with a gun specification. However, great caution needs to be exercised in how this is accomplished. For instance, many of our concealed carry provisions are felonies if violated. In fact, during the negotiations on H.B. 347, there was substantial discussion about increasing to a felony the offense of failing to notify a law enforcement officer that you are a license holder. (Despite the fact that the majority of states have no notification requirement at all.)

The easiest way to illustrate the peril faced by gun owners is with real-world examples. I was contacted on a case where a bail agent ("bounty hunter") was out working a warrant on one of his absconders. This armed bail recovery agent possessed a CHL and was engaged in the process of bringing a criminal to justice when the vehicle he was in was stopped by the police. Unfortunately, this person's handgun was allegedly in his pocket versus being IN A HOLSTER in his pocket. (At that time, the law required a holster in a vehicle if the handgun was on your person.) In addition to charging this person with improper transportation, a felony, the prosecutor obtained a gun specification, since a gun was used to improperly transport the gun. I am not making that logic up. In another case, a person with a CHL allegedly pointed their gun in an act of claimed self-defense while in a vehicle, and was similarly charged with improper transportation (for touching the gun while in a vehicle).

S.B. 184 has eliminated the possibility of charging gun specifications for crimes that already involve the possession of a firearm. For instance, improper transportation of a loaded firearm, a felony, requires the presence of a firearm to begin with. A gun specification is no longer available as an "add-on" to the indictment. However, these illustrations are still examples of the power of a gun specification. In a case with a gun specification, the first, last and only thing on the defense's mind is getting rid of the mandatory prison time carried by the gun specification. That is why gun specifications are sought, the presence of mandatory prison time virtually eliminates any possibility of a trial versus a plea offer that dismisses the mandatory prison time. Thus, your gun owner is in a no-win situation - pay ten thousand dollars and more in legal fees for a felony trial with the risk of mandatory prison time if convicted, or take a guaranteed plea to some lesser offense with no mandatory prison time.

THIS IS THE HIDDEN RISK OF CRACKING DOWN ON "GUN VIOLENCE." Anytime a law is proposed that will add additional/mandatory time for use of a gun in a crime, the Ohio gun owner needs to look very critically at just how that new law might be used against him or her should a self-defense encounter go wrong. Just one example, in 2008 a bill was introduced to add a mandatory 10 or more years in prison for anyone who uses a gun to kill a juvenile. Setting aside the logical fallacy of shooting a 17 year old being more heinous than burning them alive after torturing them, consider the situation where the 17 year old was shot in self-defense and a prosecutor

3

moves the charges forward anyway, including the new 10+ year mandatory prison sentence. This will amount to risking a life sentence for many people. Think this is an absurd "what if?" Most people thought the possibility of charging a gun specification on improper transportation was also preposterous, until shown how it happens in real life.

Attorney General Mike DeWine convened a panel to discuss potential changes to Ohio law to address "gun violence," consisting of state and federal law enforcement, prosecutors, gun advocacy groups and victim advocates. Surprisingly enough, when everyone sat down, there was broad consensus that violence is a "person problem" and not a "tool problem." Statistics in Ohio showed that less than three percent of the population, none of whom could legally own a gun, were responsible for over 2/3 of the violent felonies in Ohio. As a result, the General Assembly is, as of press time, considering a bill that would enhance sentencing for repeat violent offenders (people with two or more convictions for felonies that involved the use of deadly force).

Prosecution Process

Misdemeanors are charged by an individual swearing to a criminal complaint, which is then served on the individual charged and the case proceeds to trial. Most often criminal complaints are served on the person via summons, an order to appear in court on a certain date and at a certain time. In exceptional cases, the complaint can be served via warrant, meaning the person is arrested and brought to court. A misdemeanor complaint often looks like a traffic ticket. Misdemeanors are prosecuted in municipal/county/mayor's courts.

Felonies may not be charged by an individual, unless the individual waives the right to be indicted and instead agrees to what is called a bill of information. All felony cases that do not waive this right must be presented to the county grand jury. If the grand jury believes there is probable cause that the alleged offense occurred, they will return an indictment. The indictment is served on the individual charged and the case proceeds to trial. As with a misdemeanor, the indictment may be served via summons or warrant. Felonies are prosecuted in Common Pleas Court.

4

For all offenses above a minor misdemeanor, there is a right to a trial by jury and the right to court appointed counsel, if you cannot afford your own. For misdemeanors, the right to a jury trial must be demanded in writing. For felonies, the trial will automatically be a jury trial, unless the jury is waived in writing.

Trial to Judge or Jury

In any trial that carries the right to a jury trial, the defendant has the choice of proceeding with a jury or waiving that right and trying the case to a judge. In certain instances, it will make absolute sense to present the case to a jury and only a jury. In other instances, it will make sense to waive a jury and present the case to a judge. Only the defendant and their counsel, who is hopefully very familiar with the court, can make the decision on whether to try the case to a judge or to a jury. In almost all cases I am contacted on, I recommend the person obtain local counsel with me instead serving as co-counsel as needed, simply because it is critical to know the local court customs. The old adage that "good lawyers know the law, great lawyers know the judge" has a lot of truth behind it. Understand that I am not implying that you will get a better result if you hire the judge's golfing buddy; rather, someone who has been in that judge's courtroom for years has a leg up on someone who has never been in that courtroom.

Factors that go into whether to use a judge or jury include: the facts of the case, the nature and character of the "victim," the character and nature of the defendant, the likely makeup of any jury pool and the inclinations of the judge based upon past cases. People are fond of saying "I'd rather be judged by twelve than carried by six." My response to them is always, "You clearly have never been judged by 12." The jury process is imperfect, emotional and inherently biased by the jurors' life experiences. It isn't perfect, it is just the best process we have identified, nothing more, nothing less. As I tell people, a jury is made up of people who couldn't figure out how to get out of jury duty. I've practiced in small towns my whole life, and on several occasions I have run into people who had to sit for the jury selection process but were not seated as a juror. They will ask how the case turned out, and I can't count the number of times the other person said something like "well I figured he was guilty." These people did not hear one single piece of evidence.

Tomorrow someone might design the perfect computer to judge cases. In your particular case you might guess that the jury process, warts and all, benefits you. In another case, you feel there is no way you want a jury anywhere near the case.

Trial Process

The day of trial is going to be the second worst day of your life, guaranteed, with strong odds it might be the single worst day of your life. For almost everyone, this will be your first exposure to a criminal trial, and it sure is a lot different than what you see on TV. You will show up early in the morning after not sleeping soundly, if at all, and walk into a room full of strangers. As you walk up to the table labeled "Defendant" it will sink in, if it hasn't already, that "Defendant" means you, and you are the only one placing any betting chips on this particular table. Everyone else in that courtroom is guaranteed that, unless terrorists attack the courthouse, they will go home to their families that night.

Assuming you have not waived the right to a jury trial, the first order of business will be to select a jury. The jury selection process is referred to as "voir dire," which law dictionaries tell us comes from Old French based upon Latin. My personal lay person definition of "voir dire" is "slightly better than voodoo." During voir dire your attorney will get up and ask the jury all sorts of questions. Theoretically these questions are asked to eliminate biased persons and insure an impartial jury that will follow the judge's instructions. In reality the questions are asked to begin arguing the case and sway the jury to your side via questions like "Mr. Juror One, if some tweaked out meth addict with 15 prior convictions breaks into the sacred grounds of your home, shattering your sense of security and well-being, do you agree that it is your duty, as a man, husband and father, to protect your babies as they sleep soundly in their crib, or are you the type of nancyboy who would stand there and do nothing?"

After the judge has interrupted the attorneys repeatedly, and instructed the jury to ignore anything that amounts to argument or appeals to emotion by the attorney, and your attorney and the prosecutor feel they have sufficiently read tea leaves to determine how a juror will decide the case, you will have your jury and alternate jurors. The prosecutor presents an opening statement, your attorney presents an opening statement, and then the prosecution puts on their evidence. Once the prosecution concludes their case, it is now your turn to present your evidence.

It should be noted that you are not required to put on any defense evidence. However, in a self-defense case, it is a practical impossibility to claim self-defense without presenting evidence. (More on this later in Chapter 9.) Additionally, you are not required to testify, but, unless there is a great videotape or a bunch of eyewitnesses, it is practically impossible to prove self-defense without testifying.

After your defense case is finished, the prosecution has the chance to put on a rebuttal case – evidence strictly limited to rebutting any evidence you put on during your defense case. After the rebuttal case, the attorneys will disappear with the judge for about an hour to argue over the jury instructions. After the judge has the jury instructions, the final phase of the trial begins with the prosecutor making a brief closing argument. Your attorney then gives your closing argument. After this, the prosecutor gets to give a last closing statement, and gets the "last word" since the prosecution has the burden of proof.

The judge will then read the jury the jury instructions, and the jury will retire into jury deliberations. Thus begins the longest period of time in your life, whether it is 1 hour, 3 hours or longer, to you it will seem like forever. I personally do not put much stock in predicting how a jury will rule based upon how much time they spend deliberating – a case can be so weak that they quickly vote to acquit, a case can be so strong that they quickly vote to convict, or maybe the jury is in no hurry to get home where a pile of dirty laundry awaits them. During deliberations the jury is allowed to submit written questions to the judge. The judge will confer with the attorneys and formulate an answer, which can either be submitted to the jury in writing or conveyed verbally by the judge by bringing the jury back into the courtroom.

The jury will deliberate until they vote unanimously to convict, unanimously to acquit, or consider themselves unable to reach a unanimous decision and are "hung." If the jury is hung, the judge will send them home and declare a mistrial. The prosecutor must then decide if they want to retry the case. If the jury votes to acquit, then that is the end, and you are a free person after any processing of paperwork (i.e. booking you out of the jail if you were in jail).

If the jury votes to convict, then several things can happen, depending upon the particulars of your case. If the case is serious (i.e. involved gunshots into another human being) then you can expect that any bond you posted will be revoked, and you will be taken into custody pending your sentencing. The judge also has the ability to modify bond or waive bond, and you will remain free pending your sentencing. Prior to your sentencing, you will need to meet with a court probation officer to complete a Pre-Sentence Investigation. This is a report that is prepared and presented to the judge prior to sentencing. The report contains information on your upbringing, education, family, drug and alcohol use, your profession, prior criminal convictions, your version of the events and a sentencing recommendation from the probation department. The judge and attorneys review this report and will refer to it at the sentencing hearing. You personally will likely not see the report until the day of sentencing.

At your sentencing, the judge considers: the PSI, the statements of counsel and the victim, your statement and the sentencing factors set forth in law. At that point, you will be sentenced by the judge, with immediate execution of sentence. If you are sentenced to any incarceration, incarceration will begin immediately. In practice, there are very, very few criminal appeals that succeed, and most judges are loath to allow someone to remain free while an appeal is pending. The sentencing is the practical end of your case.

The plight of Ohio gun owners can be summarized as follows: They are among the most heavily regulated species on the planet. In order to exercise the most fundamental of human rights, the right to be free from criminal attack on their person or property, gun owners must navigate:

- Federal criminal, administrative, regulatory, and excise laws (including current attempts by the United Nations to regulate small arms), and
- State criminal, administrative and regulatory laws, and
- Editorial positions of every major media outlet, and
- The political whims of anyone who happens to hold government office.

Firearm Ownership Disqualifications

As a preliminary matter, in Ohio, a person must be at least 18 years old to legally purchase and/or posses a rifle or shotgun, and must be at least 21 years old to legally purchase and/or possess a handgun. There are limited exceptions that allow underage persons to posses these firearms when receiving firearm instruction, military/police instruction, or engaged in hunting activities.

Beyond the age restrictions, the most important laws that a firearm owner must be aware of are the laws regarding who can legally own firearms. These factors are generally referred to as disabilities; if you possess one of these disabilities, you cannot own, posses or handle a firearm. There are disabilities set forth in federal law and in state law. Not all disabilities will overlap, nor will they be the same state to state. Please keep in mind that, if a person is disqualified from owning, possessing or handling a firearm, it logically follows that they cannot be a concealed license holder, even if the concealed license law does not specifically mention that disqualification.

The Federal disqualifications are set forth in 18 USC 922(d)&(g), which state that no person may own or possess a firearm:

(1) who has been convicted, in any court of a crime punishable by imprisonment for a term exceeding one year;

(2) who is a fugitive from justice;

(3) who is an unlawful user of or addicted to any controlled substance;

(4) who has been adjudicated as a mental defective or who has been committed to a mental institution;

(5) who, being an alien:
    (A) is illegally or unlawfully in the United States; or
    (B) except as provided in subsection (y)(2), has been admitted to the United States under a nonimmigrant visa;

(6) who has been discharged from the Armed Forces under dishonorable conditions;

(7) who, having been a citizen of the United States, has renounced his citizenship;

(8) who is subject to a court order that:
    (A) was issued after a hearing of which such person received actual notice, and at which such person had an opportunity to participate;
    (B) restrains such person from harassing, stalking, or threatening an intimate partner of such person or child of such intimate partner or person, or engaging in other conduct that would place an intimate partner in reasonable fear of bodily injury to the partner or child; and
    (C) (i) includes a finding that such person represents a credible threat to the physical safety of such intimate partner or child; or (ii) by its terms explicitly prohibits the use, attempted use, or threatened use of physical force against such intimate partner or child that would reasonably be expected to cause bodily injury; or

(9) who has been convicted in any court of a misdemeanor crime of domestic violence,

The Ohio disqualifications are set forth in R.C. 2923.13. A person in Ohio cannot own, possess or use a firearm if:

(1) The person is a fugitive from justice.
(2) The person is under indictment for or has been convicted of any felony offense of violence or has been adjudicated a delinquent child for the commission of an offense that, if committed by an adult, would have been a felony offense of violence.
(3) The person is under indictment for or has been convicted of any felony offense involving the illegal possession, use, sale, administration, distribution, or trafficking in any drug of abuse or has been adjudicated a delinquent child for the commission of an offense that, if committed by an adult, would have been a felony offense involving the illegal possession, use, sale, administration, distribution, or trafficking in any drug of abuse.
(4) The person is drug dependent, in danger of drug dependence, or a chronic alcoholic.
(5) The person is under adjudication of mental incompetence, has been adjudicated as a mental defective, has been committed to a mental institution, has been found by a court to be a mentally ill person subject to hospitalization by court order, or is an involuntary patient other than one who is a patient only for purposes of observation.

If a person has one of these conditions, that person is under firearm disability and may not own, possess or use firearms. In certain limited situations, a person under disability can have their firearm rights restored. This is discussed in more detail in Chapter 13.

When All Firearms Are Prohibited

Assuming the Ohio resident can legally own/possess a firearm, this merely gets them into the next quagmire: locations that prohibit all firearms. Federal and Ohio law have several specific statutes on enumerated areas where possession of a firearm is prohibited. Please note that these statutes apply to all firearms and "open carry," and also mostly apply to licensed, concealed carry. The specific exceptions granted to concealed carry licensees are covered in Chapter 7. **This current section deals with unlicensed persons only.**

Liquor Premises: R.C. 2923.121 provides that, "No person shall possess a firearm in any room in which any person is consuming liquor in premises for which a D permit has been issued under Chapter 4303. of the Revised Code or in an open air arena for which a permit of that nature has been issued." This statute has a messy history, with prior versions using "dispense" versus "consume" while not defining what "dispense" means. The net result of the varying imprecise words and interpretations is great confusion on where this statute actually applies.

It is not as simple as focusing on the type of liquor license a facility holds, nor whether consumption is occurring. One example I like to give is as follows: the Giant Eagle in my neighborhood has a D permit and there is also occasionally consumption during taste-test events. This Giant Eagle is not a prohibited facility. The Giant Eagle 10 miles away has a D permit, but they also have a café where wine and beer is served and consumed throughout the day. This Giant Eagle is a prohibited facility. This confusion occurs because the beginning of the statute simply refers to a "D permit" yet hundreds of words later the statute specifies that D-6/D-8 permits are exempted.

For those who do not wish to dive into Ohio liquor license permit law, the best way I have come up with to describe the prohibited places is: If they are open during serving hours, can you go in, pay money, and be served a drink for consumption right then and there? If so, it is a prohibited liquor facility. For example, this covers bars, restaurants, stadiums, arenas, bowling alleys, golf courses and certain parts of hotels.

Ohio School Safety Zone: R.C. 2923.122 provides that no person shall knowingly convey or possess a firearm in a school safety zone, or convey or possess an object that is indistinguishable from a firearm. (For example, an Airsoft gun modeled after a real gun.) A school safety zone, as "defined" in R.C. 2901.01(C), includes any school premises, building or activity. Ohio does not use a "bubble" of a specific number of feet or yards from the school property, so by the plain meaning of the words the Ohio school safety zone is the school premises, building, bus or activity. R.C. 2901.01(C)(3) defines "school activity" as any activity that happens under the auspices of a school board of education. For instance, a public park becomes a school safety zone when a local high school hosts a cross-country invitational at the public park.

Federal School Safety Zone: 18 USC 922(q) establishes that, in addition to the Ohio school safety zone law, there is a federal school safety zone law, for relevant purposes set forth at 18 USC 922(q)(2) (A). The federal school safety zone is defined in 18 USC 921(a)(25) as being within 1,000 feet of the grounds of a public, private or parochial primary or secondary education school. This 1,000 foot "bubble" can prove problematic, given the amount of ground owned by schools. Luckily, there are numerous exceptions set out in 18 USC 921(q)(2)(B). These exceptions establish that the federal school safety zone law does not apply to: 1.) private property within 1,000 feet of school grounds but not ON the school grounds, 2.) persons with concealed carry licenses issued by the state (state licensing law must require a background check) the school grounds are located in, 3.) firearms that are not loaded and are in a locked container, 4.) firearms used in school activity or otherwise authorized by the school board to be present or 5.) unloaded firearms carried by those traversing school grounds to reach immediately adjacent public or private hunting grounds.

Generally speaking, what this section attempts to prohibit is firearms being brought onto school property. It is not intended to prevent a citizen, not bound for the school grounds as their destination, from passing the school on their way someplace else. As a practical matter, this law is never used unless the person possessing the gun committed some other serious crime at the time they possessed the gun in the Federal School Safety Zone.

Courthouse: R.C. 2923.123 provides that, "No person shall knowingly convey or attempt to convey a deadly weapon or dangerous ordnance into a courthouse or into another building or structure in which a courtroom is located." Sounds simple, and it is: firearms are not allowed in courthouses. Similar prohibitions apply to jails, prisons, detention centers and similar facilities.

<u>Secure Facilities: R.C. 2921.36</u> provides that no person shall convey a firearm onto the grounds of a detention facility OR institution, office building or other place under the control of the department of mental health, the department of developmental disabilities, the department of youth services, or the department of rehabilitation and correction. This is pretty broad, and means pretty any place owned or operated by these departments.

<u>Federal Offices: 18 USC 930</u> prohibits firearms in federal facilities. Generally, national parks and national forests are going to differ to, and be controlled under, state firearm laws. Federal facilities, as defined within this section, broadly means any building where federal government employees are gathered to do federal work. So any building occupied by any part of the federal government is off limits to firearm carry. There has been debate (by others) for years whether this includes post offices. Yes, it does. Clearly. That was my opinion 11 years ago, it is my opinion today, and it is affirmed by at least one federal appellate court. (<u>U.S. v. Dorosan</u>.)

<u>Possession of Firearm While Intoxicated: R.C. 2923.15</u> prohibits possession of a firearm while intoxicated (under the influence of drugs or alcohol). Further, R.C. 2923.16(D) establishes a separate, felony level offense for possessing a firearm in a vehicle while intoxicated, even by a passenger. There is great misconception in the public mind about "under the influence" and what is allowed or prohibited. Although 0.08 BAC is established as being under the influence for DUI, that does not mean that there is a "free pass" up to 0.08 BAC. A person can be, and usually is, under the influence below 0.08 BAC. Plenty of DUI prosecutions happen with a breath test below 0.08 or with no breath test at all. There is no safe, "allowed" level of alcohol in your system before you are legally considered under the influence. I have included the jury instruction defining "under the influence" in Appendix A for you to review. I would stress that one or two beers is probably not going to trigger "under the influence" legally, but that third or fourth beer has the potential to be the most expensive beer you have ever consumed.

"Open" Carry

The Ohio Supreme Court, in <u>Klein vs. Leis</u>, and in <u>Cleveland v. Arnold</u> previously, examined the right of an individual to carry arms in the context of a challenge to Ohio's concealed carry ban. The court upheld Ohio's ban on concealed carry and found that there is no right to carry a concealed weapon. The court also reaffirmed that there is a fundamental, individual right, under the Ohio Constitution, to carry arms, as had been the case prior to <u>Klein vs. Leis</u>. These state-law decisions predated the <u>Heller</u> and <u>McDonald</u> SCOTUS decisions.

The first major problem with holding out the <u>Klein</u> and <u>Arnold</u> cases as implying that open carry is 100% legal is that the court did not strike down any state or local law prohibiting the open carrying of firearms. For example, the law prohibiting open carry in a motor vehicle was upheld in <u>Klein</u>. Further, ordinances banning mere ownership of broad classes of firearms, such as "assault weapons" in the <u>Baskin</u> case, were upheld. It is difficult, and risky, to look to cases banning categories of conduct as authority allowing that same conduct.

The people who argue that open carry was affirmed in those cases do so under an analysis that involves a right established by implication, as was examined by the Ohio Supreme Court in the predatory lending cases. Establishing something by implication means, basically, that because A-V are prohibited, W, X, Y and Z must be legal and therefore a right. In plain English, (too late I am sure) those arguing for legal open carry by implication felt, 1.) The Court held that bearing arms is a fundamental, individual right under the Ohio Constitution, 2.) It is not a violation of this right to ban concealed carry, 3.) The only remaining method to exercise this right is through open carry, 4.) Therefore open carry is legal. Turning to our current world in Ohio, we now have an alternative method of exercising that right available, a CHL, so this argument is even weaker now than it was in the pre-H.B. 12 days. Additionally, almost 100% of courts considering the scope of the right have thus far limited the constitutional right to self-defense to existing only within the home or place of business.

The single strongest authority for open carry being legal in Ohio is R.C. 9.68, which says that Ohio citizens "without further license, permission, restriction, delay, or process, may own, possess, purchase, sell, transfer, transport, store, or keep any firearm, part of a firearm, its components, and its ammunition" unless specifically prohibited by state or federal law. Specifically included in this statutory right EXPLICITLY is the carrying of firearms, openly or concealed. See R.C. 9.68(C)(1). This statutory grant does not rely upon case law or court interpretation; it is a plainly worded grant of a right, which also accomplishes displacement of a city's power to further regulate the exercise of this right. R.C. 9.68 has twice been upheld against cities by the Ohio Supreme Court.

While open-carry laws may put police officers (and some motor-cyclists) in awkward situations from time to time, the Ohio legislature has decided its citizens may be entrusted with firearms on public streets. Ohio Rev. Code §§ 9.68, 2923.125. The Toledo Police Department has no authority to disregard this decision—not to mention the protections of the Fourth Amendment—by detaining every "gunman" who lawfully possesses a firearm. Shawn Northrup v. City of Toledo Police Dep't, et al United States Court of Appeals for the Sixth Circuit (2015).

Open carry is statutorily legal in Ohio, except in areas that are covered by specific state or federal statutes that ban firearms. See the discussion of these areas above. Note that areas prohibiting open carry are covered by the specific "no gun" statutes above, and not the no-carry areas set forth in CHL law, discussed in Chapter 7. An unfortunate result of this is that Ohio has areas where licensed carry of a concealed handgun is legal but open carry is illegal, and areas where open carry is legal but licensed carry of a concealed handgun is illegal.

A final note on open carry: Ohio is not a mature state when it comes to firearm laws, especially open carry. Just because something is legal does not mean that the participant is free from potential arrest and/or criminal charges. The time, and expense, of proving yourself right will be borne by you. Ultimately, charges against an open carrier like "disorderly conduct" or "inciting panic" are not going to stick, if the open carry conduct was peaceable conduct. I personally get very afraid and panicked when I realize that a person needs a valid driver's license to buy Sudafed at the pharmacy but only needs a utility bill to vote for President. My panic or discomfort that arises from my own fears and prejudices about the exercise of their right to assemble, organize and vote does not turn their lawful conduct into unlawful conduct. For a court to rule otherwise would be equivalent to ruling that I cannot visibly and peacefully exercise my rights without facing criminal prosecution due to someone else's irrational fears.

You need to understand that being right after the fact is not always satisfying. In one instance, I was involved in a case where a person was confronted (felony stop) for walking from his own front door to his own car while carrying openly. The police department ended up issuing an apology and requiring revised training for all officers, advising them that open carry was legal. The department was also gracious and professional in an interview with The Dispatch by admitting a mistake had been made and steps were taken to make sure the mistake was not repeated. This does not diminish what this man and his wife went through. Similarly, some high-stakes, high-stress encounters have happened in northern Ohio when concerned citizens have called the police on open-carriers. I deeply fear someone is going to get shot prior to the police departments getting "up to speed" on this issue.

Transportation of an Unloaded Firearm In a Motor Vehicle

Ohio has specific laws on the transportation of a firearm. The actual statute, R.C. 2923.16, is fairly straightforward and is easy to comply with. In summary, four methods are provided to unlicensed persons for the transportation of a firearm. All four methods require that the firearm be unloaded.

This is the portion of the book where we used to spend several pages talking about how convoluted Ohio's definition of "unloaded" had become, courtesy of case law defining "loaded" to mean basically "ammunition anywhere in the vehicle." S.B. 184 returned sanity to transportation of firearms in Ohio, and there is now a clear, easy to understand, statutory definition of "unloaded." Now, "unloaded" is defined in R.C. 2923.16(K)(5). In summary, a firearm is unloaded if:

-   there is no ammunition in the firearm being transported, and
-   there is no ammunition in a magazine or speed-loader for the firearm being transported, or if
-   there IS ammunition in the magazine or speed-loader for the firearm being transported, the magazine is stored in a compartment reachable only by leaving the vehicle, or the magazine is stored in a container that "provides complete and separate enclosure of the magazine from the firearm."

Breaking this definition down, we see that a gun is unloaded as long as there is no ammunition in the firearm, and no ammunition loaded in magazines or speed-loaders in the vehicle for that firearm. En bloc clips and stripper clips are specifically defined to NOT be a magazine or speed-loader. A container that "provides complete and separate enclosure of the magazine from the firearm" is defined via convoluted language that I did not write. Basically, the magazine containing ammunition would have to be in an enclosure that <u>closes via a snap, buckle, zipper, or hook and loop or other fastener that must be opened</u> and is outside the compartment of the container containing the firearm. i.e. outside magazine pouches on a rifle case, a stand-alone mag carrier that closes, in one of your pockets that closes etc. I can't even begin to tell you how many hours were wasted coming up with this compromise to allow rounds in magazines in a car.

So after you have met the definition of "unloaded," you now get your choice of four methods to transport your unloaded firearm:

-   unloaded and in a closed case, package or box; or
-   unloaded and in a compartment reachable only by exiting the vehicle; or
-   unloaded and secured in a gun rack that is in plain sight; or
-   if the firearm is a long-gun, unloaded and in plain sight with the action stripped open, or if the gun has no action, unloaded

and in plain sight (long-gun is defined to mean overall length of at least 24 inches and barrel length of at least 18 inches.)

Most modern vehicles do not have a compartment reachable only by leaving the vehicle. Pass-through rear seating, folding rear seats, SUVs and mini-vans have made this mostly a thing of the past. Also note that an 18 inch barrel is required to use the long-gun method – there are perfectly legal rifles with under 18 inch barrels that most people would consider long-guns, yet do not meet the criteria to use the plain sight method above.

The moral of this story is "have a gun case." If the gun is unloaded, and the gun is in a closed gun case, end of discussion. It doesn't matter where the gun case is, and it doesn't matter where the ammunition is, so long as the firearm meets the definition of unloaded. If you do have ammunition in a magazine/speed-loader, then you get to navigate the separate enclosure language. Keep in mind that if you are confused, the police are also likely confused and you might experience some excitement, and hassle, if you wind up in a traffic stop.

Keep in mind that the above section controls unloaded transportation only; licensed transportation of a loaded handgun is dealt with later in this book. However, the licensee needs to keep in mind that their license covers handguns only, not shotguns and rifles. This means the unloaded transportation methods discussed above are the only way to transport rifles and shotguns.

Mandatory Attorney Fees

Under prior law, if the police wrongfully withheld your firearm from you, you were faced with spending $2,000 or more on a court case to recover a $500 firearm. This, unfortunately, has been a recurrent problem in Ohio, particularly anywhere near Cuyahoga County and in Marion County. S.B. 184 changed the law to provide for a mandatory award of attorney fees to anyone who has to sue to recover their firearms. If a gun owner makes a "final demand" from the police (return the firearm or I will sue) and the police refuse to return the firearm, and the owner sues and the court orders return of the firearm, the court "shall" award you your reasonable costs and attorney fees. See R.C. 2923.163.

Also, R.C. 9.68 has a mandatory attorney fee provision. This means that municipalities that choose to disregard clear state law establishing that their ordinances are no longer valid will need to write an attorney fee check to anyone who challenges their blatant, unlawful disregard of state law. Under prior law, the municipality had no motivation at all to abide by state law. See Chapter 16.

This is an important change to "even the playing field" in these situations. In every single instance I have been involved in, the police/municipality has zero incentive to proactively look at the case critically and return the firearm or amend their ordinances. Instead, the attitude has been "sue us." Now, with attorney fees awarded, it is more likely police will look closer at returning the firearms and municipalities will consider amending their ordinances. As of the writing of this book, shenanigans still abound, with the most frequent being the police running background checks on persons prior to returning the gun and/or requiring proof of lawful ownership of the gun. (Sales receipt etc.) At most it results in a headache for a day or two and with the assistance of counsel communicating with the Prosecutors, the games stop and the gun is returned. Further, some places are playing brinksmanship with their "no gun" signs. When push comes to shove, the signs come down.

Apartment Eviction

Prior law allowed a tenant to be evicted simply for exercising the constitutional and statutory right to posses a firearm in his home. S.B. 184 put an end to this. For any lease agreement entered into after September 9, 2008, tenants WHO HAVE A CHL may no longer be evicted for peaceably and lawfully exercising their right to own a firearm. (See R.C. 2923.126(C)(3)(b))

A Note on Prepositions

Over the past seven years, students, usually fellow motorcycle riders, are fond of pointing out that all of Ohio's motor vehicle restrictions deal with people riding IN a vehicle, whereas a person rides ON a motorcycle. I am aware of two cases where motorcycle riders have tried to hide behind the preposition – one conviction and one hung jury, and I don't know if the hung jury case was re-tried. Considering the felony consequences for failure and the virtual certainty that any court is going to decline to place significance on preposition choice, please consider yourself IN a motor vehicle when you are riding ON a vehicle.

A Note on Plurals

Not too long ago a trainer behind the lines in the People's Republic of Cuyahoga County passed along that the prosecutor up there has taken the position that a concealed carry license in Ohio only allows the carry of a single handgun, based upon the numerous instances of the phrase "a handgun" in our code. "A" handgun clearly refers to the singular.

R.C. 1.43(A) (Rules of Construction, Singular – Plural) states that within the Revised Code the singular includes the plural and the plural includes the singular. A court might want to ignore that statutory interpretation rule based upon anti-gun prejudice, but it is the statutory law in Ohio since 1972.

It is important to understand that Ohio does not have a concealed weapons license; it is a concealed <u>handgun</u> license. Thus your license does not cover shotguns, rifles, knives and other similar lethal tools. Concealed carry of deadly weapons in Ohio is illegal. R.C. 2923.12(A) (1) establishes this prohibition, and the Ohio Supreme Court upheld it in the <u>Klein</u> case. There is no constitutional right, under federal or state constitutions, to carry a concealed deadly weapon. Anyone who wishes to conceal and carry a deadly weapon, other than a handgun, must rely upon the affirmative defenses to a charge of carrying a concealed weapon (CCW). These are the same affirmative defenses that existed prior to our handgun licensing law, the same defenses that proved largely unsatisfactory and essentially worthless. These affirmative defenses are available after the person is arrested, charged, and prosecuted, and have <u>to be proven by the defendant at trial</u>.

The affirmative defenses are:

1. The weapon is carried for defensive purposes while at work or going to and from work, and that work is of such a nature that a prudent person would go so armed, or
2. The weapon is carried for defensive purposes while the carrier is engaged in a lawful activity and the carrier has reasonable cause to fear criminal attack upon himself or herself or a family member such as would justify a prudent person going armed, or
3. The weapon is carried for any lawful purpose while within the four walls of the person's home.

Since this section of the Ohio Revised Code applies to all "deadly weapons" except licensed handguns, the old affirmative defenses are still on the books for non-handgun "deadly weapons" throughout the Revised Code. Ohio's concealed carry license is for handguns only, and does not apply to other "deadly weapons."

It is extremely important to note that Ohio has created a special exception in weapon laws for handguns, which now have their own license and regulations. Thus, these affirmative defenses, which are available for other deadly weapons and do not apply to handguns. Only licensed persons may carry a concealed handgun.

Here is an easy bar bet for you to win. Ask a buddy, "What is the definition of an illegal knife in Ohio?" Chances are people will start guessing blade lengths, opening mechanisms and other similar characteristics. The correct answer is, "A knife is illegal in Ohio if it is carried as a weapon." Yes, you read that right, it is a subjective test. Ohio's statute simply states, "No person shall knowingly carry or have, concealed on the person's person or concealed ready at hand, any of the following: A deadly weapon..." (See R.C. 2923.12(A) (1)) What is a deadly weapon, you ask? "Deadly weapon" means any instrument, device, or thing capable of inflicting death (See R.C. 2923.11(A)). A half-inch blade on a pen knife can inflict death.

To further compound the problem, Ohio does not have "deadly weapon" preemption; rather, Ohio has "firearm" preemption. Thus, all of the municipalities are still free to have their own knife laws, and many do. This is where all the arbitrary blade-length restrictions come in. The moral of this story is that no person in Ohio should carry a concealed deadly weapon, other than a handgun pursuant to a valid license, unless they are willing to take great risk, and great expense, to prove the affirmative defenses at trial. Personally, if I carry a knife, it has a bunch of packing tape residue on it to show I carry it to use as a tool, not a weapon.

H.R. 218, Nationwide Law Enforcement Carry

The United States Congress passed H.R. 218 in 2004. This law establishes nationwide concealed carry for law enforcement officers, regardless of local department policy or foreign jurisdiction laws. This law is found at 18 USC 926(B), right after the nationwide unloaded transportation of firearm laws, found at 18 USC 926(A). Neither statute is reproduced in this book.

In brief, qualifying law enforcement officers may carry a concealed "firearm" that has moved in interstate commerce. This specification is made because Congress does not have general legislative powers, so the fiction is that this law regulates interstate commerce, one of the explicit, enumerated powers congress does have. In order to fall under this law, the person must be a "qualified law enforcement officer" and cannot carry firearms anyplace where state law restricts carrying firearms on private property through trespassing laws, nor anyplace where state law restricts carrying firearms in/on government property/buildings.

Stated another way, those carrying under H.R. 218 still must abide by private property owners posting "no gun" signs and must abide by state law if state law prohibits carrying of guns in/on government property/buildings. An off-duty officer in Marion, who was seeking medical care at an Urgent Care in Marion that had signs posted, learned this lesson the hard way and at gunpoint. The only exception would be if the law enforcement officer was actively involved in police business (i.e. on duty on a call or working court papers). The old fiction of "always on duty" is not recognized under H.R. 218 or Ohio law. Ohio's trespass statute, R.C. 2911.21, contains no law enforcement officer exception.

The best way to describe a "qualified law enforcement officer" for H.R. 218 purposes is some person with arrest powers who is involved in the investigation or prosecution of crimes and who is authorized to carry a firearm during their duties. Further, persons retired from these positions after at least 15 years service may carry under 18 USC 926(C), so long as that person has a photo identification from their agency indicating their retired status, and so long as that person has, in the prior 12 months, fired and passed the standard police qualification course of fire as determined by that state. In both cases, the officer or retired officer cannot carry a machinegun or firearm silencer.

The post-concealed carry license law in Ohio still holds that carrying a concealed handgun is illegal, there is no constitutional right to carry a concealed handgun, and there are no longer "prudent person" affirmative defenses for carrying a concealed handgun. Thus, if you want to carry a concealed handgun, you must get a Concealed Handgun License that is recognized in Ohio.

Ohio's CHL is implemented through the General Assembly creating a special category of laws for licensed carry of concealed handguns. This results in Ohio having laws that apply to all deadly weapons, laws that apply to all firearms except handguns, and laws that apply to handguns only. Then, for non-firearm deadly weapons, add back in the local regulation of all other deadly weapons, due to the lack of preemption for deadly weapons other than firearms. This results in a real messy mix of weapon laws in Ohio.

Take Ohio's law prohibiting a CHL from carrying a concealed handgun into a house of worship, unless the house of worship has "opted in" and allows concealed carry. If that CHL:

- Enters into a church with a concealed handgun, and the church HAS NOT "opted in," they are committing a felony CCW violation.
- Enters the same church with a concealed handgun AND a knife in their pocket, and the church HAS "opted in," the handgun is legal but the knife is illegal and they are committing a misdemeanor CCW violation under state law, and perhaps also under local ordinance.
- Enters the same church with an AR 15 slung over their shoulder, and the church HAS NOT "opted in," and has also posted "no guns" signs on the church doors, they are committing a misdemeanor trespass violation.
- Enters the same church with an AR 15 slung over their shoulder, and the church HAS NOT "opted in," but hasn't posted any no gun signs at all, they aren't violating any

firearm laws. (I wouldn't recommend doing this, you'll get the chance to pay an attorney to prove it wasn't illegal.)

I can't make this up. Four scenarios involving the same CHL and the same facility, three scenarios result in crimes, all of them different, yet the fourth scenario is legal.

Ohio's license is a "shall issue" system: so long as the gun owner is qualified under the statute, they are entitled to a license. The gun owner does not need to justify the reasons behind applying for a license. The only exception is the Temporary Emergency License (TEL), in which case the gun owner has to show evidence of imminent danger in order to justify the immediate issuance of the license. (This will be examined in Chapter 6.)

Due to the long, adversarial nature of the concealed carry law, a lot of compromising was done to secure passage of the original bill and subsequent "fix up" bills. These compromises have left gun owners with exactly that, a compromised law. The theory expressed by the sponsors passing the original bill was "camel's nose": Get one part of concealed carry into Ohio's tent and the rest can follow, be fixed or be improved later.

In 2006, H.B. 347, the first improvement/fix bill, passed over Governor Taft's veto. It was, and still is, the first and only veto-override in Ohio in nearly 40 years. Content-wise, H.B. 347 was very important. Clearly the most important content of H.B. 347 was firearm preemption as set forth in R.C. 9.68. H.B. 347 did make other, minor improvements to firearm laws, but it also increased penalties for "status-offense" violations like failure to notify a police officer you have a firearm and failure to obey a police officer. Indeed, the FOP and State Patrol opposed this bill and insisted that failure to notify an officer or failure to obey an officer ("contempt of cop") be increased to felonies. Despite the fact that law enforcement officers were gaining clear benefits and exemptions within this bill, the status quo "downtown" was that in order to obtain improvements, new, increased penalties must also be approved. Two steps forward, two steps back.

This is why the importance of H.B. 347 is not reflected merely in the bill's content. Behind the scenes, a seismic power shift occurred. Until this bill, it was necessary to remove objections from the FOP and State Patrol in order for a bill to pass. During the June 2006 deliberations on H.B. 347, we were told, point blank, that we had to accept making contempt of cop a felony to move the bill. This was what was necessary to remove law enforcement objections, and Governor Taft will veto the bill if law enforcement objects. Take it or leave it. This was the ultimatum, despite the fact that law enforcement had not demonstrated any need to create these new felonies. Clearly this was political horse trading, nothing more.

We said "no thanks." Actually, the message was, in part "In summary, we cannot accept any framework that views concealed carry reform as a zero-sum game. If it is the Senate's position that law enforcement groups have a de facto veto, and their position remains that we must make our law worse any time we make it better, then we have profound problems."

Late October of 2006, a new (fifth draft) of the bill was circulated, and the exact same ultimatum was delivered. This new draft still contained the two new felonies, and it was clear that the Senate was simply trying to protect Governor Taft from an embarrassing veto showdown. Thanks to the over-whelming support and pressure applied by gun owners, we knew we had the votes. On October 30, 2006, we once again said "no thanks." The bill passed the Senate a month later. As we were told later, this was the first time a group had stood up to the FOP and Ohio Highway Patrol, and won. This continues to pay dividends to this day.

S.B. 184, which went into effect in September of 2008, was really the most sweeping "reform" type of law any state has seen. In terms of content, this bill was staggering. Numerous improvements went into effect, and not a single new "status offense" or increased penalty was included. The State Highway Patrol, now under Governor Strickland, did not oppose any of the bill, and the FOP's objections were largely easy to overcome. There was one final sticking point, however, and the way it was overcome is a story worth sharing.

May 16, 2008, I was attending the NRA annual meeting in Louisville, KY. While I should have been there to enjoy the meetings and receive the 2008 Defender of Justice Award, I actually spent most of my time on the cell phone hammering out the last details of S.B. 184. There was, unfortunately, an impasse in the House over the last few improvements to be included. The next day, Saturday the 17th, was the big banquet, and I had great seats due to be being an award winner (Chris Cox's family sat with me, which was very generous of Chris.) Thanks to this generosity, I was talking to a Congresswoman about the impasse. Her response was "Didn't Governor Strickland already say he'd sign that?" When I replied yes, she pulled out her cell phone and called a well known conservative talk radio host, who then invited the parties in question onto his show to talk about why Ohio House Republicans were holding up a pro-gun bill that a Democratic Governor said he would sign.

S.B. 184 was passed by the House on May 28, 2008, less than two weeks after that phone call. Sometimes it is hard work, sometimes it is blind luck, and sometimes it is just being in the right place at the right time.

The "backstage" stories on the two recently passed bills, S.B. 17 and H.B. 54, will have to wait for several years so that the people involved can maintain their privacy. I figure four years is a good, arbitrary period of time to pass before I publicly tell any stories. Even then, some confidences will continue to be kept.

Every person who is considering concealed carry of a handgun in Ohio has a duty to themselves, the public and the concealed carry "community" to know: how to safely handle and carry a firearm, how to safely and accurately employ a firearm, the rules regarding the use of force and, when in doubt, be prepared to do nothing. There have been far too many negligent discharges of firearms by licensees not properly carrying their gun, and at least two shootings that will be "poster child" cases for the gun banners as we move forward. Balance those instances against the dozens of reported cases of valid self-defense shootings by licensees and the over 460,000 people carrying on an Ohio license, and the mistakes seem small in context. (After all, police officers commit crimes and negligently discharge firearms.) While we accept these as small in context, editorial boards couldn't care less about accuracy or fairness in reporting in context. Any incident that happens will have the media play them for all they are worth in pursuit of their anti-gun agendas.

Outside of large urban population centers gun violence is very rare. Some rural school districts in Ohio still have deer season or hunting season days off from school. Just a decade ago it wasn't unusual for a high school student to check a gun in at the principal's office in the morning to go hunting before or after school, yet school shootings were unheard of. Ohio was one of the last states in the nation to adopt a licensed concealed carry system, and 11 years later all 50 states have some form of lawful concealed carry. The editorial policies of Ohio's major newspapers are anti-gun and anti-concealed carry, and these same newspapers previously published license holders' personal information as a thinly veiled intimidation tactic. It took a change in the media access loophole to shut down this abuse and intimidation. Not a single list of gun owners has been published since this change in the law.

CHAPTER 5. COMPETENCY CERTIFICATIONS

Ohio's system for CHLs (Concealed Handgun Licensees) provides that the applicant must have training prior to applying for the CHL. Members of the military and retired military, who have received prior equivalent training, may use that training to apply for a CHL. An applicant who has completed the Ohio peace officer training may use that training to apply for a CHL. An applicant for a TEL (Temporary Emergency License) does not need to have any training prior to applying, under the rationale that the TEL is only good for 90 days and is only granted in emergencies. If the holder of a TEL wants to get a permanent CHL, he/she will have to obtain the required training prior to applying for his/her CHL. There are multiple methods available for satisfying Ohio's training requirements, and the applicant only needs to satisfy one of these methods.

The acceptable competency certifications are:

1. Complete a firearms safety, training or requalification or firearm safety instructor class offered under the auspices of a national gun advocacy organization, or
2. Complete a firearms safety, training, requalification or safety instructor course that:

   • Was open to the public, and
   • Was taught by an Ohio Peace Officer Training Commission certified instructor or an instructor certified by a national gun advocacy organization, and
   • Was offered under the auspices of a law enforcement agency, college or firearms training school, or

3. Complete an Ohio Peace Officers Training School and have a certificate from said school, or
4. Be an active or reserve member of the armed forces, honorably discharged member of the active or reserve forces, or retired law enforcement officer, if he/she can certify that the duty training he/she received was equivalent to the training required under the Ohio competency certification requirements, or

5. Have a certificate from a course conducted by an instructor certified by a government entity or a national gun advocacy organization that complies with the requirements for Ohio competency certification, or
6. Have an affidavit from the instructor of his/her competency certification class attesting to the successful completion of said class.

A person relying upon gun school training must apply within 3 years from the date on their training certificate. There is no longer a requirement that gun school training be renewed every 6 years. For discharged or retired military who are relying on their military training to apply for a CHL, the training must have occurred within 10 years of application. The Ohio Peace Officers certificate has no date restrictions.

All competency certification classes taught in Ohio must have at least 8 hours of instruction, broken down as follows:

1. 6 hours of classroom training on the rules of safe gun handling and proper storage practices, demonstration and explanation of how to handle ammunition and demonstration and explanation by the student on how to handle ammunition and handguns, and
2. Have the student demonstrate the knowledge, skills and attitude necessary to shoot safely, and
3. Involve 2 hours of range time and live fire training where the student demonstrates the applied use of the knowledge gained in the classroom training, and
4. The class must have a written examination on the topics covered in the class.

A recent change in Ohio law now allows for completion of a portion of part, or all, of the classroom hours via online training. CAUTION: Ohio law requires that online training meet the same requirements as classroom training and include an interactive component i.e. something to prove the person was actually at the computer. You will still have to find an instructor who is willing to accept this online training and then take you to the range for 2 hours and sign a competency certificate. There is nothing that requires instructors to do so. Further, with all of the online training I am aware of, there will be no way the range instructor, or the sheriff you submit your CHL application to, can verify the training met these requirements. I expect lots of trouble with online training.

CAUTION: Ohio law did not define what a national gun advocacy organization is. Bloomberg's various groups are all national gun advocacy organizations, for example. It is up to the sheriff to determine if they will accept the credentials of your instructor. You will always be safe if you use an NRA or law enforcement instructor.

Please understand that minimal compliance with the competency law is not necessarily something you should aspire to. Shooting is a perishable skill. Even instructors who are teaching these classes weekly need to "sit on the other side of the lectern" occasionally. Find new, interesting training and eagerly attend it. Advanced training is going to be far different than the initial 8 hour training, and chances are high that you will enjoy it greatly. I personally try to attend advanced training at least every other year. I have found that, given my teaching schedule, I seldom get to the range as the shooter. Signing up for advanced training forces me to keep my skills current.

In order to obtain a concealed handgun license (CHL) or a temporary emergency license (TEL), an applicant must go through a defined process that involves multiple steps. As this information is contained in several different portions of the Revised Code, and does not lend itself to a narrative presentation, the information will be presented in an outline format instead.

The Ohio Peace Officers Training Commission is to develop and make available to sheriffs:

1. The actual form for the license that will be issued by all 88 sheriffs, said license form to contain the following information:

    • Name, address, date of birth and color photo of the licensee, and
    • Date of issue of the license, date of expiration of the license, county of issuance, the sheriff's name, the county ID code and the unique license number, and
    • The signatures of the licensee and sheriff issuing the license.
    • Note: The law specifically prohibits the recording of a gun serial number on the license. (i.e., this is not a "per gun" license).

2. The form for temporary emergency licenses, and
3. Procedures for processing and issuing licenses (Note: The Attorney General of Ohio has issued a non-binding opinion that an applicant does not need to provide a social security number on the application.), and
4. A pamphlet explaining dispute resolution, all aspects of use of deadly force, and make these pamphlets available to persons or entities operating training courses. (The Ohio Attorney General will review the pamphlet and recommend changes as needed.)

The actual application form is developed and maintained by the Ohio Attorney General's office. Note that the standard CHL form now contains a second section, which is intended to be used only by people who are requesting a law enforcement sign-off for a NFA item. More on this in Chapter 15. If you are applying for a CHL only, you only need to fill out the CHL section of the application.

Application Process

1. Fees for licensing:

    • A resident of Ohio for five years or more will have to pay an application fee equal to the actual cost of issuing the license or $67.00, whichever is less.
    • For all other persons, the actual costs of the FBI background check plus the lesser of the actual cost of issuing the license or $55.00. (Currently a total of $91.00.)

2. An application for a CHL may be turned into the sheriff in the applicant's county of residence or the sheriff of any contiguous county. Sheriffs are allowed to, and most do, require appointments to process applications. This generally is not a problem, but in response to some obstructionist counties having very limited hours, it is a legal requirement that applications of any kind be accepted at least 15 hours per week, and the hours must be posted. An application for a TEL may only be turned in to the sheriff in the applicant's county of residence, and the Sheriff must accept these emergency applications without an appointment at any time during normal business hours.

3. Upon receipt of the application and supporting materials, the sheriff is to:

    • Perform a criminal record check, and
    • Perform an incompetency record check, and
    • Perform a NICS record check (the same check that is done when you buy a gun from an FFL.)
    • The criminal record check is to be done by electronic fingerprinting where available. Where electronic fingerprinting is not available, a traditional fingerprint specimen card will be obtained and sent to the Ohio Bureau of Criminal Investigation and Identification (BCI) for the criminal record and incompetency check. For those who have lived in Ohio less than five years, the FBI background check process will be used instead.

- There is a limited right of appeal to challenge inaccurate records or information that the sheriff may obtain/find.

4. The application materials to be presented to the sheriff include the following:

- The actual application, and
- The fee for application, and
- A color photo taken within 30 days of the day of the application, and
- A competency certificate or documentation, and
- The fingerprint specimens through whatever media that sheriff supports, and
- A certification that the applicant has read the pamphlet prepared by the Ohio Peace Officers Training Commission concerning dispute resolution and use of force. (Note: the application contains this certification at the bottom of the application.)

5. Theoretically, the sheriff has 45 days to act from the date of receipt of the application materials. If the sheriff has not received information indicating that the applicant is disqualified from license issuance within those 45 days, the sheriff shall issue the license. I say "theoretically" because even though the law specifies the sheriff has 45 days and shall issue on or before the 45th day, there is little to do to force strict compliance by the sheriff AND there is a conflicting provision of law (R.C. 2923.125(D)(3)) that mandates that the sheriff "shall suspend the processing" of the application if the sheriff becomes aware of an arrest or charge for a disqualifying offense. The very likely result of trying to force compliance on day 45 will be the sheriff denying the application on the basis of the information in hand (usually an old entry in LEADS showing an arrest or charge for a disqualifying crime, but no indication if a conviction resulted), and forcing the applicant to appeal while the sheriff completes whatever is taking more than 45 days to investigate. If one county develops a pattern or trend of consistently exceeding 45 days, we will be able to get a court to address this. For the one or two people who go past 45 days

on rare occasion, the unfortunate reality is they are really stuck without effective remedy.

6. The law provides for the issuance of a TEL on an "immediate" basis. The process is:

- The application requires a sworn statement (the Ohio Supreme Court, in the Josephine Lee case, ruled that the sheriff has no discretion in reviewing the content of the sworn statement i.e. the applicant need not satisfy the sheriff of the reasonableness of the sworn statement; mere conclusory statements are good enough) that the applicant fears imminent attack on his/her person or a member of his/her family, or
- The application requires written documentation from a governmental entity describing the facts that the applicant is basing his/her sworn statement upon (for instance, an application for a civil protection order or police report), and
- A sworn statement from the applicant containing the same information as is contained upon the standard application form.
- The emergency license is valid for 90 days from the date of issuance.
- There is no competency certificate requirement for the issuance of an emergency license.

Regular and Emergency License Eligibility

1. As far as qualifications, the applicant must:

- Be in the United States legally and a resident of Ohio, and
- Be at least 21 years of age on the date of the application, and
- Not be under indictment or charged with a FELONY drug offense, a misdemeanor offense of violence, negligent assault or a violation of Ohio Revised Code Section 2923.1211 (This section deals with altering a concealed carry license or being in possession of a license that has been revoked.), and
- Not (ever) have a conviction for a felony, a felony drug offense or assault when the victim was a law enforcement officer, and
- In the last 3 years, have no convictions for misdemeanor offenses of violence, and

- In the last 5 years, have no more than one conviction for assault or negligent assault, and
- In the last 10 years, have no convictions for resisting arrest, and
- Not be an adjudicated mental defective, and
- Not be a subject of any protection orders issued by this or another state.
- Note that Ohio no longer "counts" against an applicant a conviction that has been sealed or from which an applicant that has been restored to firearm rights.
- Ohio now has specific provisions for the military with regard to their residence being in Ohio even if they are temporarily stationed elsewhere, and also for those in the military temporarily stationed inside of Ohio. The military members will no longer face objections to their "residence" being in Ohio in either circumstance.
- Ohio now allows military members over 18 years old to purchase a handgun but the minimum age for issuance of a CHL or TEL remains 21 years old.
- Ohio law now allows for issuance of a "non-resident" license to someone who works in Ohio but has their residence in another state. This type of application must submit their application to the sheriff in the Ohio county where they are employed or an immediately adjacent Ohio county. (Note: Ohio now accepts any concealed carry license from a non-resident, so this provision probably will rarely be utilized.)

2. The actual application requires that you provide the personal information required for the license, answer questions about all of the statutory disqualifiers, and list, to the best of your knowledge, all addresses where you have lived since the age of 18. If you have difficulty in recalling all of your prior addresses, go to www.annualcreditreport.com and pull your own credit report for free without any obligation to sign up for screening programs or similar scams. At the end of the credit report will be a section listing every address the credit bureau has ever had for you. Basically, anyplace you have ever received a bill.

3. NOTE: Ohio's law does not mention that there is a Federal firearm disability for domestic violence convictions. The application

asks about a domestic violence conviction, so this is assumed to be a disqualification based upon federal law.

4. If the sheriff denies the license, the sheriff must specify in writing the reasons for denial, and there is a limited right of appeal from this denial.

5. If the sheriff becomes aware of any fact that would constitute a disqualifier during the processing of the application, the sheriff must suspend processing until that fact is resolved.

6. Please note the discussions in Chapters 1 and 2: Just because a person can legally own a firearm does not automatically equate to the person being eligible for a license. Also, just because someone is eligible to get a license does not mean the person can legally own a firearm. The General Assembly is allowed to place whatever restrictions on this license privilege they deem necessary.

7. An offense is created for making false statements in an application for a concealed carry license and for submitting false documents in support of an application for a concealed carry license.

Denial of an Application

1. The law provides for limited appeals from a decision by a sheriff denying an application. These are set forth in R.C. 2923.125(D)(2)(b)&(c) and 2923.127.

   - R.C. 2923.127 deals exclusively with challenging a criminal record found during the criminal record check, and establishes the procedures for challenging these questioned records. This would most often be utilized in a situation where a conviction for a "John Smith" was showing up on another "John Smith's" criminal record.

   - R.C. 2923.125(D)(2)(b)&(c) is the merit appeal process, to be used when the applicant feels the sheriff's denial was contrary to law. This appeal process appears to be limited to denials based upon the criteria listed in 2923.125(D)(1), but it is also purportedly the appeal process for a denial of a TEL under 2923.1213.

   - R.C. 2923.125(D)(2)(b) specifies that appeals from a denial based upon one of the criteria in 2923.125(D)(1) are to be conducted under R.C. 119.12. This is a statutory appeal process established to cover appeals from administrative hearings, and other processes that are specifically made subject to R.C. 119.12. This process requires compliance with the explicit procedures outlined, and must be commenced within 15 days of the denial. It is strongly recommended that an attorney file this appeal for the denied gun owner.

2. If a Court sustains the denial of an application, the applicant must wait one year prior to reapplying. The law does not specify any waiting period prior to reapplication for a denial that is not appealed, but presumably the applicant will have to wait for the disqualifying factor to be remedied.

A few, final observations on applications and denials. All 88 sheriffs seem to be participating in the process in good faith. There is an occasional report of an application taking over 45 days to process, or of a sheriff giving out bad information on a student's instruction being unacceptable, but for the most part this has been a pain-free licensing system. There almost certainly will be problems as online training is rolled out and the sheriffs try to determine what instructors, other than NRA and law enforcement, qualify as instructors certified by a national gun advocacy organization. Demand for the license remains strong and constant, with over 460,000 Ohio valid licenses currently being carried as of second quarter 2015.

Chapter 7. Carry Regulations

This chapter MUST begin with a cautionary note on reciprocity and foreign jurisdiction recognition. Ohio's law allows for the Attorney General to enter into reciprocity agreements with other states. Reciprocity is a process where states enter into a formal agreement wherein each state recognizes the other's license. This is compared to recognition, wherein a foreign state recognizes another state's license without the need for a formal agreement or quid pro quo. See Appendix B for reference resources to check on reciprocity and recognition.

The most important thing to remember is that if a gun owner is carrying in a foreign jurisdiction, they are bound by that state's laws and regulations. Thus, someone carrying in Ohio on an out of state license will be bound by Ohio's laws. Ohio license holders carrying in another state will be bound by that state's laws. THE VISITOR TO OHIO IS STRONGLY CAUTIONED TO BE ON THE LOOKOUT FOR SIGNS, AND TO KNOW THE PROHIBITED CARRY PROVISIONS IN DETAIL.

Ohio's regulations on concealed carry of a handgun present a maze of compliance issues. Again, given that the restrictions are spread throughout the law, the best presentation of this material is obtained by the following outline format.

General Prohibited Areas

1. All of the "no gun" areas covered earlier in Chapter 2 are still "no gun areas." In addition to those "no gun areas" having separate, dedicated statutes, Ohio's concealed carry law has restated these areas in R.C. 2923.126 as off-limits to concealed carry, to make sure there is no confusion as to a CHL now being permitted to carry in these areas. There are limited exceptions granted to licensees to enter into these "no gun areas" and these are discussed below in the specific prohibited areas section.
2. R.C. 2923.126(C)(3) allows the owner of private land, or a private person leasing public land, to post no-guns signs. The right

of the private property owner trumps any exception in the concealed carry law. This applies equally to concealed and openly-carried firearms.

- There is no requirement in Ohio for the wording, the size or the placement a no-gun sign. Rather, the test is "would a reasonable person be placed on notice" by the sign.
- If the property posted is primarily a parking lot, it is not a criminal offense to be on the land, and instead the property owner must use civil trespass remedies.
- A violation of posted signage or other warnings will not be a license violation per se, but rather a criminal trespass violation under R.C. 2911.21. This applies even to off-duty law enforcement, as H.R. 218 and Ohio's trespass statute make no exception or provision for off-duty law enforcement.
- It is perfectly legal for a private property owner to post a sign that bans firearm possession by the general public and then grant specific individuals the right to be armed, on-premises, and this does not invalidate the sign.

Specific Prohibited Areas

Ohio's concealed carry law creates what I refer to as three categories of prohibited areas. There are the private property prohibited areas that exist simply because someone posts a no-gun sign. These are discussed above. Then there are areas that are general no-gun areas (all firearms), and concealed carry is only allowed in these general no-gun areas if specific exceptions are granted. Finally, there are areas that are not no-gun areas, but your concealed carry license is not recognized in these areas (CHL specific). (i.e. a church – not a "no-gun" area but your license is not recognized there, unless the church "opts in" to concealed carry.)

The law establishes 10 categories of specific no-carry areas that apply to CHLs and TELs. A license holder cannot, absent specific exception, carry a loaded concealed handgun in the following 10 categories of places:

- In a police station, sheriff's station, highway patrol station, BCI office, jail, prison, detention facility, work house, airport, state mental institution or institution for mental retardation.

- In a school safety zone. SEE DISCUSSION OF EXCEPTION FOLLOWING THIS SECTION
- In a courthouse. SEE DISCUSSION FOLLOWING THIS SECTION
- In premises where liquor is consumed for which a D class permit has been issued. SEE DISCUSSION OF EXCEPTION FOLLOWING THIS SECTION
- On the property of a public or private college or university, unless the firearm is locked in a vehicle or immediately in the process of being placed in a locked vehicle. Note that a college or university IS NOT a school zone under Ohio law. Note that this law is specific to licensed concealed carry. There is no state law banning guns on the property of a public or private college or university.
- On the premises of a house of worship, unless there is a posted policy allowing concealed carry in the house of worship. Note that this law is specific to licensed concealed carry. There is no state law banning guns in a house of worship.
- Upon the premises of child daycare centers, including home daycares. Note that this law is specific to licensed concealed carry. There is no state law banning guns in a child daycare center.
- In private or commercial aircraft.
- In buildings that are "government facilities" owned by the state or any political subdivision of the state. This prohibition section now explicitly excludes (allows concealed carry in) buildings that are primarily bathrooms, parking facilities, shelters or rest facilities. "Government facility" means places where government employees gather to do government work. This was modeled on the federal office statute.
- In any place where federal law prohibits the carrying of firearms (post office, ATF office, IRS office, all the areas talked about in Chapter 2 18 USC 930).
- There is a requirement imposed upon persons controlling the properties described above to post signage warning people that their property is one of the prohibited properties. Lack of signs is not a defense to arrest and being charged.

1. Private employers may still ban firearms from their premises and private property. This could mean, for instance, that an employer's parking lot is not posted with a sign, yet an employee could still be fired for having a firearm locked in their vehicle.
2. Private employers are not required to adopt a policy one way or another on the issue of concealed carry.
3. Private employers are given qualified immunity from civil liability related to their policy decisions with regard to banning or allowing concealed carry on their premises, unless the employer had a malicious purpose in deciding the policy. Additionally, private employers are specifically granted absolute immunity for any claim related to their policy decision to allow, or ban, licensed carry on their premises.
5. Political subdivisions are granted civil immunity arising from the acts of licensees on their property.

THE SCHOOL SAFETY ZONE EXCEPTION granted to someone with a CHL is narrow and defined. If the licensee is a "passenger" or "driver" "in a motor vehicle," then the person may enter the school safety zone immediately in the process of picking up or dropping off a child. R.C. 2923.122(D)(4). Please note that the "exception" set forth in R.C. 2923.122(D)(3) is a legal impossibility and can never apply. Thus, the only school zone exception is for licensees who are in a vehicle immediately in the process of dropping off a child. Here are the potential "traps." First, if there is an unloaded shotgun in a case in the trunk, you don't meet the exception because your CHL applies to handguns only, and the exception is CHL specific. Second, if the school calls and says you child is sick and you need to come pick him up, you will have to leave the car to go into the office and sign the child out. You cannot meet this exception because you will not be "in" a vehicle. You must drive home and drop off your handgun, then go pick up your child. Third, this exception applies to drop off or pickup of a child only. There is no provision to drop an adult (i.e. your wife the schoolteacher) off.

THE COURTHOUSE EXCEPTION granted to someone with a CHL is problematic and probably exists nowhere in Ohio. The courthouse may provide a "gun check" to allow a licensee to leave a handgun in the custody of the courthouse security officer. This "gun check" provision would apply to state/county/municipal courts and not federal courts. There are several problems with this. First, the court is not required to provide gun checks. Second, the court can, by local rule, prohibit all persons from conveying weapons into the courthouse. Third, The Supreme Court of Ohio can, by rule of superintendence, prohibit the conveying of weapons onto courthouse grounds. Fourth, the gun owner will have no way of determining whether a courthouse has a gun check station in operation or not prior to being well within courthouse grounds. This exact scenario has already resulted in the arrest of a license holder who was asking where the gun check station is located.

THE LIQUOR FACILITY EXCEPTION granted to someone with a CHL provides that the liquor facility statute, R.C. 2921.121, does not apply to a licensee so long as the licensee does not consume any alcohol (not even a sip) while in the facility, and is not already under the influence of drugs or alcohol when entering the facility (facility with a class D liquor license when consumption is occurring). Please note that this is an exception, not a grant of a right. The exception simply says R.C. 2921.121 does not apply in that instance. The private property owner can still post a no-guns sign and trigger a criminal trespass violation under R.C. 2911.21. The signs that are posted that begin with "Warning, if you are carrying a firearm…." (usually printed on white cardboard stock, black lettering) are not "no-gun" signs but are statutory warning signs required by R.C. 4301.637. It would be a legal absurdity to say that these signs trigger a trespass violation, because such an interpretation would require a court to find that the exception passed by the General Assembly cannot ever apply. Stated another way, the general assembly passed a specific exception within R.C. 2921.121 to allow someone with a CHL to carry into a liquor facility, yet every single liquor facility is required by law to post this sign under R.C. 4301.637. Would the general assembly intend to pass an exception that could never apply because of R.C. 4301.637? Absurd.

Liquor licensees (i.e the people that own the restaurant) who have a CHL may have a handgun at their own licensed premises for defensive purposes. Liquor licensees also have the ability to hire armed security as needed. As with any other private property owner, a liquor licensee may post a no-gun sign to keep the public disarmed, but then authorize individuals to carry a handgun despite the no-gun sign.

Concealed Carry Regulations Not Related to Prohibited Areas

1. You may carry a handgun, or any other deadly weapon, concealed on your person, within your own home without a license, so long as you are not otherwise prohibited from having the deadly weapon. This also applies to having the deadly weapon concealed but not on your person within the house. This is both explicit (R.C. 2923.12(C)(1)(d)) and an affirmative defense for non-handguns (R.C. 2923.12(D)(3).)

2. A concealed carry license holder must carry the CHL and other state-issued photo identification on their person at all times while carrying a concealed, loaded handgun.

3. A concealed carry license holder must notify in writing the sheriff that issued their license of a change of address within 45 days of any move.

4. If a person is arrested for concealed carry of a handgun and "promptly" produces the license to carry a concealed handgun, the police officer "shall" not arrest the person. See R.C. 2923.12(F) (2). As further specified in this same section, if the licensee does not produce a license at the time of encounter, the licensee may be arrested, even if the officer can independently verify the existence of a valid license. The penalties for failure to have your CHL or TEL on your person vary according to how long it takes to produce your license. See R.C. 2923.12.(F)(2)(a), (b) and (c.)

5. The various levels of penalties imposed for carrying a concealed handgun are largely based upon factors that are not covered by these materials. For instance, I can easily demonstrate that if a person carries a handgun (openly or concealed) into a drycleaner posted "no guns," they are committing a simple criminal trespass. I can also easily lay out a fact pattern that the same person could face charges for breaking and entering or burglary. If you have to worry about the different levels of penalties, chances are good that you have already been charged criminally, and you need to obtain competent counsel to assist you with your case.

Loaded, or "Concealed" Carry in a Motor Vehicle

A person with a valid CHL may transport a handgun in a motor vehicle (so long as they are not under the influence of drugs or alcohol) in any manner they choose R.C. 2923.16(F)(5). Having said this, there are other ways to get into trouble. Access control would be the number one issue. There has been at least one instance where the CHL left the gun laying in the open and a child in the car got ahold of the gun and fired it. This would not be an improper transportation issue, rather, it would be somewhere along the lines of illegal discharge of a gun from inside a car or endangering children

Common sense is the number two issue. If the handgun is simply laying on the front seat, and the CHL has to slam on the brakes, or gets into an accident, Newton tells us that handgun is going to continue traveling along the vector it was traveling on and at the speed it was previously traveling. Now the handgun is slamming into the dashboard at 35 mph. Guns are designed to be drop safe, not collision safe. Now maybe the gun fires. Or maybe the gun goes into an airbag that is exploding. Now you have a 2 pound steel projectile traveling around the inside your car as a result of an explosion that exceeds 150 mph.

LAW ENFORCEMENT INTERACTION

If the driver or the occupant of a motor vehicle is a license holder and is transporting his/her loaded handgun in compliance with the above, and the vehicle is stopped for a law enforcement purpose, or, if the licensee is subjected to a pedestrian stop, commonly referred to as a "Terry Stop," the license holder must:

- Promptly inform any law enforcement officer that he/she has a license for concealed carry and is carrying a loaded firearm (Note: Any vehicle that is registered to a CHL holder is going to be flagged at the time of the traffic stop by the Law Enforcement Automated Data System (LEADS). Make sure that people borrowing vehicles/spouses are aware of this. Additionally, it would be very good practice to observe the following steps, EVEN IF NOT CARRYING, as the officer is going to know you are a CHL holder and expecting you to act a certain way. If you are not acting that way, tensions will rise.), and

- Comply with all orders of all law enforcement officers at the scene, and
- Remain in the vehicle, unless instructed to do otherwise, and
- Keep hands in plain sight at all times during the stop (assume this is "10 and 2" on the steering wheel, dashboard, window-sill or low surrender), unless instructed to do otherwise, and
- Not touch the handgun at all, unless instructed to do so by the officer. (Note: Officers can legally take possession of the handgun for the duration of the stop, but MUST return it at the conclusion of the stop. GET EXPLICIT INSTRUCTIONS ON HOW TO ACCOMPLISH THE TRANSFER OF POSSESSION OF THE HANDGUN!)

Failure to notify is invariably brain-freeze from a licensee who is under stress or just not knowing about the duty to notify. Remember folks, when you sign that application, you are certifying you've read the AG's booklet, which explains in very clear detail that you are required to notify the officer, and that you cannot touch the handgun. Still, the instructors are to blame for licensees failing to comply with this law. If their students are not walking out of class with the traffic stop requirements tattooed on their eyeballs due to the repetition and emphasis, the instructor is failing the student.

Every other area of our training involves repetitive practice and role playing. We go to the range, we practice draws, we practice reloads etc. We do this because training makes reactions automatic, and under stress we do not think properly about what we should be doing. Thus, we want our reactions to be appropriate when we are no longer able to think clearly. Dealing with the police is a stressful situation, and if you have not practiced for this scenario, you should not expect to perform any better than the person who has never practiced a reload and is now trying to reload in the dark with an intruder somewhere in the house. PRACTICE DEALING WITH THE POLICE. Every pay-day or the last Friday of the month, make it your practice day and practice traffic stops in your garage or parking lot. Have your spouse role play the police officer if needed. Practice every possible variation. The first time to try the "song and dance" should not be at the side of the road after a violent car crash.

Ohio's concealed carry law provides for the issuance of a replacement license upon the submission of an affidavit stating that the license holder lost the original license.

Ohio's license can be renewed by filing an application for renewal of the license within 90 days prior to the expiration of the current license or anytime after the expiration of the current license. In applying for a renewal, the applicant must submit a new photo and certify a rereading of the pamphlet issued by the Ohio Attorney General. The renewal applicant is not required to submit a current competency certification and new fingerprint specimens. The renewal fee is $50.00, because the sheriff will only check your background back to the date of your last license issuance, not all the way back to age 18 as is done with your initial license application.

A concealed carry license is good for five years from the date of issuance, with a 30-day grace period after the date of expiration. (See R.C. 2923.126(A)).

The issuing sheriff may suspend or revoke a TEL or CHL. A suspension is used upon the arrest or beginning of a court case that could result in a disqualifying condition for the licensee (i.e., a protection order is filed for, arrest for assault) and continues until the court case is resolved in the applicant's favor. R.C. 2923.128(A)(2) provides a mechanism for the sheriff to also suspend your license for convictions that are not otherwise license disqualifications. For instance, failing to promptly notify an officer during a traffic stop that you have a handgun is not a disqualifying conviction, but it is a conviction that will suspend and/or revoke your license for a period of time. R.C. 2923.128(A)(2) provides the sheriff the means, and the requirement to, suspend your license for these convictions related to disregarding obligations placed upon you as a license holder. This will, undoubtedly, encourage Ohio citizens to get CHLs from other states rather than Ohio, so they do not have to worry about their license being suspended for violations of obligations that other states do not even impose.

A revocation occurs upon a license holder being convicted of a disqualifying offense, a protection order being issued against the license holder, or upon the sheriff otherwise becoming aware of the holder being disqualified under applicable law.

If a license is suspended or revoked, the sheriff is to notify the licensee by certified mail. It is a crime to be in possession of a CHL or TEL that has been suspended or revoked.

Please bear in mind that a CHL suspension is not the only way to deny your right to carry a firearm for self-defense. Any non-firearm related crime can carry up to five years of probation, and it is a valid term of probation to prohibit the probationer from possessing any firearms during the term of probation. While this is not a "license suspension" by the court or the sheriff, that is a distinction without a practical difference.

The law on self-defense and use of deadly force is very well established and stable. The basic premise of self-defense is that a law abiding citizen with "pure heart and clean hands" should not have to suffer an attack on his/her person without legally being able to resist that attack. Conceptually, self-defense accomplishes this in one of two ways. The first way, which Ohio does not use, is what I summarize as "negate the intent." Ordinary criminal statutes punish the decision to commit a criminal act, not the act itself. This is the reason that we do not criminally convict 10 year-olds or the insane; they are unable to appreciate the wrongfulness associated with the criminal decision. (My summary for laypeople; all lawyers and law professors please stop rolling your eyes.) This approach to self-defense says that the person did not make a decision to commit a crime; rather, they were merely reacting based upon how the attacker acted, in essence forcing the person to choose to act in self-defense. Society has chosen to allow people to decide to act in self-defense. There was no criminal intent, there was no crime.

The other approach, which only Ohio uses (law books refer to this approach as "the Ohio rule"), is to treat self-defense in as a general affirmative defense. An affirmative defense can be specific, such as defenses contained within our individual weapons statutes i.e. our concealed deadly weapon statute. In these cases, the specific defense is laid out within the statute, and is only available to someone charged under that statute. An affirmative defense can also be general, such as entrapment or self-defense. That is to say, it is an affirmative defense to any criminal charge and is not listed within any particular statute. Self-defense could be a general affirmative defense to a felonious assault charge, but it also could conceivably be a defense to a littering charge. Thus, even though someone might violate several criminal statutes in defending a car-jacking (touching the gun in a car, shooting from a car, felonious assault etc) the claim of self-defense is a defense to any crime you committed in the course of defending yourself, not just pulling the trigger.

The important distinction between the two systems is that when there is no criminal intent, there is no crime; whereas with an affirmative defense, a criminal offense necessarily occurred and the actor is not disputing the elements of the charge, and instead is disputing conviction based upon the defense. Stated another way, the actor is not disputing that s/he did x, y and z, and is instead saying "yes I did do x, y and z but it was justified based upon the following...." KEEP IN MIND THAT UNDER THIS SYSTEM, ANYTIME YOU ACT IN SELF-DEFENSE YOU NECESSARILY ARE STARTING WITH THE COMMISSION OF A CRIME AND YOU ARE CONFESSING TO THE CRIME.

One court summarized it nicely: "Self-defense is not merely a denial or contradiction of evidence offered by the state to prove the essential elements of the crime charged, but rather is the admission of prohibited conduct coupled with claims that surrounding facts or circumstances justify the conduct."

The practical problem with the Ohio rule is that unless there is a video tape of the encounter, or a bunch of credible, reliable eye witnesses, the person acting in self-defense will be forced to give statements and/or testify at their trial in order to prove their case. We all know we have the right to remain silent and that you cannot be compelled to testify during your criminal trial. Well, the Ohio rule is forcing a choice upon you: either you can remain silent, or you can claim you were acting in self-defense. In most instances, you won't be able to exercise both rights.

Before examining self-defense in detail, I want to be candid that what follows is my summary of self-defense law. Self-defense law in Ohio is mostly case law, and in order to present a coherent, complete yet accessible explanation, I have summarized some nuances into broad statements. Ohio Jury Instructions on self-defense are fair guides for a summary of self-defense law, but the instructions ARE NOT the law. So, for instance, the first part of the self-defense test generally is referred to (within case law and jury instructions) as the person was not "at fault in creating the situation." The body of case law has held, in various places, that a person is not at fault in creating the situation if they are not the aggressor, did not prolong the situation, and did not escalate the situation (disproportionate force used in response). Rather than qualifying and explaining that "creating the situation" means a bunch of different things, it is easier to just summarize all that is encompassed in the body of case law is included via this summary.

In general, to establish non-lethal self-defense, a person must show that:

1. The person was not at fault in creating, prolonging or escalating the situation that gave rise to the need to exercise self-defense, and
2. The person had reasonable grounds to believe and had an honest belief that s/he needed to use the force that was used in defense of self or property.

Step one above, not creating, prolonging or escalating the encounter, reduces down to never being an aggressor. You cannot start the fight, if the other person tries to abandon the fight you cannot chase him/her down to continue the fight, and you cannot escalate the fight (disproportionate force used in response). If any of that does occur, you are considered the aggressor from that point forward and cannot claim self-defense.

Unfortunately, the law cannot nicely define the exact level of force that may be used. The analysis is something of a force spectrum – one extreme would involve resolving the dispute through arbitration, while the other extreme would involve using lethal force. A person may only use the amount of force that is reasonably necessary to repel the attack on his person or property, and no more. A person may not needlessly escalate the force involved in an encounter.

It is important to understand that non-lethal force may be used to defend property; lethal force may never be used to defend property. In one example, if someone steals your car keys off a table and jumps into your car to leave, you are limited to non-lethal force. If, however, that person sticks a knife in your face and says "give me your car keys" that is a threat to you, not your car, and lethal force is back on the table if all other elements are satisfied.

In looking at whether a reasonable degree of force was used, a jury would be instructed to place themselves in the defendant's shoes, literally and figuratively, with his/her particular physical character- istics and experiences, medical conditions, gender, age, training, martial arts experience etc and with his/her knowledge; then the jury would decide, based upon all of that, whether the defendant used a reasonable degree of force.

"Reasonable grounds to believe" basically means objective facts. What are the facts? If there was a security camera video, what would it show? The attacker was male, mid-20s, about 6'00", 180#, the victim was male, late 60s, about 5'3", 200#, they're in alley, it is dark etc. "Reasonable grounds" means the objective fact picture you were faced with.

"Honest belief" means that in your mind and in your shoes, any reasonable person would reach the conclusion that your fact picture amounted to a threat.

In looking at whether a person is justified in using self-defense, threatening words alone will never justify the use of force or deadly force. Resort to such force is never justified by abusive language no matter how provocative. In deciding whether a person employ- ing self-defense had reasonable grounds to believe and an honest belief that use of self-defense was necessary, juries are instructed to put themselves in your position, with your characteristics, your knowledge or lack of knowledge and under the circumstances and conditions surrounding you at the time you exercised self-defense. A further test of reasonableness is also looking at whether excess force was used. If the force used is so greatly disproportionate to the apparent danger as to show unreasonable purpose to injure the attacker, then self-defense is not available.

Up until now, it has been the absolute rule that a jury can only con- sider self-defense if a judge allows them to consider self-defense.

It is entirely discretionary, and the courts have unanimously upheld this approach. First, I think that approach is now in question, since Heller specifically held that there is a constitutional right to self-defense. I don't see how a discretionary system will survive a world where self-defense is a right under the U.S. Constitution.

Second, even in cases where the judge goes squirrely, there is still a jury standing between you and the jail. I have literally read transcripts where the judge instructed the jury "this is not a case of self-defense and you may not consider it as such." Yet the jury found the defendant Not Guilty, which should have been an impossibility given the evidence was clear. There is a jury verdict that I summarize, only half-jokingly, as "Some People Just Need Killing," which is really the jury nullifying the case because they don't care if the conduct was illegal or not, they agree with the results. A thin hope to be sure, but for some it is the only hope left.

Audiences are fond of trying to get me to commit to an opinion about a "what if" scenario, and usually have the same success in pinning me down as someone trying to nail Jello to a shower curtain. The only honest answer that can ever be given is: If on that day in that courtroom in front of that fact-finder you can convince them that the test was met, then it is a good case of self-defense. If you don't, then it wasn't. Every criminal practitioner has had a "good" case go "bad" and vice-versa.

The law on self-defense also states that a person may exercise self-defense on behalf of a third party if that third party is unable to do so on their own. In this scenario, you can only exercise self-defense on behalf of another person to the same extent that person could have used. Third party self-defense presents numerous pitfalls, and should be used with extreme caution. You almost certainly will not be privy to the totality of the circumstances for the altercation that you are observing, and it is quite possible that you can end up employing "self-defense" against a non-aggressor who is actually defending himself or herself from attack. For example, you see someone grappling with another person and you use force against that person, and it turns out that person is an under-cover store detective making a shoplifting arrest. All you have done is commit assault, and you will have no defense since you weren't defending yourself and the person you did defend has no valid claim of self-defense.

It is important to emphasize that you should avoid third party self-defense whenever possible, and only then utilize force to the extent that would be justified by the person you are defending. Understand that you will only be able to claim self-defense if the person you defended could properly claim self-defense.

CHAPTER 10. LETHAL/DEADLY FORCE IN SELF-DEFENSE

When looking at the level of force used, self-defense involves a level of reasonableness: you cannot use a howitzer to defend against a mosquito. This is particularly important when examining self-defense in light of employing the use of <u>deadly force</u>. (Please note that the terms "deadly" force and "lethal" force are used interchangeably and without distinction.) Prior to employing deadly force in self-defense, a person must show that he/she:

1. Is not at fault in creating, prolonging or escalating the situation giving rise to the need to employ deadly force, and
2. Had reasonable grounds to believe and an honest belief that they <u>were in immediate danger of death or great bodily harm</u>, and that their only means of stopping the attack was by the use of deadly force ("last resort"), and
3. Has not violated any duty to physically retreat.

What is set forth above is almost word for word from <u>State v. Robbins</u> 58 Ohio St.2d 74. (The court actually refers to the person acting in self-defense as "the slayer." "The slayer is not at fault....") The first, and most of the second, prong of this test were discussed in Chapter 9 and will not be repeated here. The only new things added in the second prong are "imminent danger" and "last resort."

Looking at these three criteria, it is important to note that they are sequential steps. That is to say, if you were at fault in creating the situation giving rise to the need to use deadly force, it does not matter what your belief was and what your opportunity to retreat was. You will have extreme difficulty in establishing self-defense, as you have not met the first prong of the test. Similarly, if you were not at fault in creating the situation giving rise to the need to use deadly force, <u>but you did not have</u> an honest belief that you were in immediate danger of death or great bodily harm, or did not have reasonable grounds to believe that you were in immediate danger of death or great bodily harm, you will have trouble in attempting to justify the use of deadly force as a means of self-defense, as you failed the second prong.

It is also important that the gun owner understands two important facts when looking at employing lethal force in self-defense. First of all, lethal force is never justified in the defense of property. Human life is infinitely more valuable than property. This is distinguishable, however, from the scenario where your personal safety is threatened by someone wanting to obtain your property. There is a vast difference between watching someone steal your unoccupied vehicle out of your driveway and someone pointing a knife at you and demanding the car keys. One is a pure property threat, the other is a threat to your safety.

"Imminent danger" is simply some objective fact in your fact picture that would cause a reasonable person standing in your shoes to conclude that the attacker was about to use deadly force against you.

The law abhors the taking of a human life, and the burden is on the individual to avoid the necessity of taking a human life whenever possible. This is also known as the use of force being a "last resort." You are not going to have to take a stupid risk to stop the attack. For example, you would not have to pick up a chair to try and beat a guy with a gun senseless.

Even if the first two prongs of the self-defense test are met, and lethal force would in all ways be justified, you still must retreat from the situation if you are able to do so safely in order to avoid the use of deadly force in defense of yourself. You do not need to subject yourself to unreasonable risk of injury in order to retreat, but keep in mind that one of the first things that is going to be examined by the police/prosecutor looking at your case is whether you could have reasonably avoided the necessity of using lethal force in self-defense by leaving the confrontation.

The duty to retreat comes from the 1500's in England. It is outdated and out of place in our modern world with modern weapons. Yet Ohio in the past 10 years had a trial and appellate court decision that held that a person had a duty to retreat from a locked jail cell prior to killing his cellmate. You just can't make this up.

There is no duty to retreat in your residence (See e.g. R.C. 2901.09, State v. Williford 49 Ohio St.3d 247, State v. Peacock 40 Ohio St.

333), business (See e.g. <u>Graham v. State</u> 98 Ohio St. 77) or personal vehicle (vehicle owned or leased by that person or that person's immediate family member) (See R.C. 2901.09). Please note that this does not mean that you can shoot someone within your residence, business, or personal vehicle with impunity; rather, it indicates a much lower threshold to meet the test of whether or not you can employ lethal force in self-defense or not. Simply put, there is no duty to retreat in your home, your business, or your personal vehicle, but the rest of the test still applies. (Please see following section on Castle Doctrine for the definition of residence.)

I have heard countless times variations of "If you shoot someone on your porch, just drag them inside the door and you will be OK." While these comments are made in jest, it is obligatory in a book of this nature to explicitly state that this simply is not true. Leaving aside Castle Doctrine for the moment, all that changes in your home, your business, or your personal vehicle is the duty to retreat. The first two steps of the test are still very much in play, and if you can't prove one of the other two steps, you still have a problem. For instance, if you disproportionately respond and/or you provoked the encounter, the general lethal force self-defense test is not going to excuse your conduct, whether you are inside the house or not.

A SPECIAL NOTE ON BRANDISHING, SHOOTING TO WOUND, WARNING SHOTS AND SIMILAR HALF-MEASURES. You do not shoot to warn, wound or kill. You shoot to stop a threat. If you shoot once and miss, and the bad guy curls into the fetal position and wets his pants, that was a great shot. If you punch someone's ten ring 4 times and they still stab you, you didn't get the job done.

Prosecutors have another term for warning shots: attempted felonious assault, improper discharge of a firearm etc. Shooting someone in the leg rather than center mass is similarly misguided and will not evade serious felony charges. Similarly, pulling out a gun just to "defuse the situation" is a legal non-starter. Do not be tempted to do this. If the gun comes out of the holster, the gun owner had better be justified in immediately employing it fully. There is no such thing as a warning shot or shooting to wound. This will be construed as a miss, bad marksmanship and perhaps even attempted murder.

I understand the theory that the presence of a firearm might eliminate a confrontation. However, the opposite is equally true. For illustration purposes, assume the following: Someone was rudely and dangerously cutoff on a street, the horn blast that logically followed developed into the "cutter" getting out of the car to go yell at the "cuttee." The "cutter" does not display anything other than bare hands. Unfortunately, "cuttee" then displayed his handgun in the honest belief that it would avert/end the confrontation. Bad move.

First, no threat of imminent serious physical harm or death had been made, thus the person who took out the handgun did not have any legal justification for using lethal force. Second, the "cuttee" has escalated the situation: Within his own car, without any threat of serious physical harm or death, he removed a handgun from a holster. This action clearly, in this circumstance, could be construed as a threat. Would the "cutter" now be justified in drawing a handgun of their own and shooting the "cuttee," assuming it wouldn't violate a duty to retreat? This scenario will always present more questions than answers, and the gun owner is going to be playing against long odds if he brandishes a firearm in a non-lethal situation.

Removing a handgun from a holster, or even possibly just uncovering and indicating the presence of a handgun, can be considered a hostile act and will be considered a criminal act. As the old saying goes, an armed society is a polite society[1], and people do not need to be waving guns around to accomplish this. IF YOU ARE GOING TO TAKE YOUR HANDGUN OUT OF A HOLSTER, YOU HAD BETTER BE LEGALLY JUSTIFIED IN USING IT IMMEDIATELY.

Readers, students and the general public never like this answer, but I assure you it is an accurate answer under Ohio law and has withstood the test of time and appellate cases. Any deliberate action on your part that introduces lethal force into the encounter in a manner that makes the other person aware of the lethal force, IS THE USE OF LETHAL FORCE. If you make reference to lethal force, show

---

[1] Robert A. Heinlein, *Beyond This Horizon*

lethal force, hold lethal force in your hand etc., those actions are simply an alternative use of lethal force, short of pulling the trigger. If you are in a non-lethal encounter, and have used lethal force, even in this round-about, alternate way, you have escalated the encounter and will have difficulties proving your self-defense case.

A SPECIAL NOTE ON "CASTLE DOCTRINE." Ohio has adopted Castle Doctrine, and the law is in force as of September 2008. See R.C. 2307.60 and R.C. 2901.05. The first critical thing to understand about "Castle Doctrine" is that "Castle Doctrine" is a marketing term, not a legal term. No two states have the same version of Castle; rather, they have a package of civil and criminal reforms under the heading of "Castle Doctrine."

The package of reforms focuses on two broad areas. First, there is an elimination of the duty to retreat. This invariably is called "stand your ground" or "make my day" depending upon who is doing the spinning. The duty to retreat is a relatively recent introduction in America; for much of our early history there was no such thing, and the concept was derided. While the duty to retreat is somewhat innocent appearing, it has its true roots in England, in the days of highwaymen and swords, not gang bangers and crack. Ohio recently had a case where the jury was instructed that there was a duty to retreat from a locked jail cell, and that case had to go all the way to the Ohio Supreme Court before there was a recognition that perhaps that instruction was absurd.

Second, the package introduces a presumption against the bad guy. In our current system of affirmative defense, the burden of proof is on the person acting in self-defense. In essence, you are guilty until you prove yourself innocent if you shoot someone in self-defense. By creating a legal presumption against the bad guy, the law changes so that someone acting in self-defense now cannot be charged criminally, or sued civilly, if the bad guy was committing a violent act against them at the time.

This is the general concept of Castle Doctrine, and each state decides how much, or how little, of the idea they embrace.

Ohio's specific version of Castle Doctrine made two broad changes, one civil, one criminal. The civil reform, which is not self-defense specific, is easy to understand and simple to summarize: If you are harmed while you are committing a felony or a misdemeanor that involves violence, whether you are charged with a crime or not, you have no civil cause of action against anyone for the harm you suffered. Stated another way, if you are committing a crime and get hurt, it is your own damn fault.

Ohio's Castle Doctrine criminal law change is more nuanced and sophisticated. The best description I have come up with is as follows: If you are lawfully in a residence or in a motor vehicle, and someone trespasses or attempts to trespass into that residence or vehicle, then you are legally presumed to be properly acting in self-defense, including lethal force, until the prosecution proves otherwise. (All words mine, not exactly recited from the statute.)

Take a look at R.C. 2901.05 and then let's take a moment to break down and examine the seven critical elements within my summary.

LAWFULLY IN…you are present lawfully. You haven't trespassed, violated a protection order, or committed a crime while you are there. (Note that the statute actually specifies that the person acting in self defense must not be present unlawfully. I summarize that as being present lawfully rather than using the double negative. However, since the statute does specify "not unlawfully" this does leave a wide door open for a court to determine the full scope of "unlawfully" in the residence or vehicle. For instance, someone selling pot from their vehicle isn't trespassing into that vehicle, but can we conclude they are unlawfully in their vehicle, since they are committing a crime from within the vehicle?)

A RESIDENCE…residence is really a concept more than a fixed place. It can be a house, it could also be a tent during the night, a hotel room, an R.V. parked for the night or a friend's house, but at the same time it isn't the detached garage or barn on your own property. Residence largely equates with the concept of domicile in the law. The easiest lay summary is to say "Residence=place where you will sleep." See R.C. 2901.05(D)(2) and (3) for actual definitions

A VEHICLE..."motor" vehicle is not specified, simply "vehicle," which roughly means some conveyance designed to transport people or cargo with or without a motor. Also, unlike the duty to retreat language, there is no restriction

TRESPASSES INTO...the person against whom the force is used has no right or privilege to be present in the residence or vehicle. A person cannot be "trespassing" if they have a right or permission to be present, and can only "trespass" when they do not have a right or permission to be present.

ATTEMPTS TO TRESPASS INTO..."attempt" is not defined within Castle, but adequate legal definition abounds. Simply put, "attempt" means some action that if successful is reasonably calculated to lead to some result. Someone lifting up a car door handle is "attempting" to enter into your car; someone knocking on your car window is not.

LEGALLY PRESUMED...the law now says that from the first moment that you were properly acting in self defense until they prove otherwise. (I refer to this as the "Castle presumption.")

UNTIL PROVEN OTHERWISE...Ohio's system is a "rebuttable presumption" meaning you get the initial presumption unless it can be overcome, in this case, by a preponderance of evidence. For instance, if the bad guy was in your occupied house and was confronted, then turned around to run out the front door and you shot BG three times in the back, you might have a problem. Similarly, if it is an 8 year old Cub Scout selling popcorn who came in through an open door, you have a problem. The facts can bite you in the behind and overcome the presumption, and then you are back to a straight self-defense trial. Strictly speaking, the statute says the prosecution may only overcome the presumption by proving the person who used the force was not lawfully present and/or proving that force was used against a person who was not, in fact, trespassing or attempting to trespass. I foresee juries and/or judges introducing their own ways to overcome the presumption if it involves the 8 year old Cub Scout.

The biggest area of confusion I have run into is that YOU MUST BE IN THE RESIDENCE OR VEHICLE for the Castle presumption to apply. If you come home and find your home broken into and the burglar leaving, you have no Castle presumption. Similarly, if you saw them inside and THEN entered, you have no Castle presumption. If you see someone stealing your unoccupied vehicle, you have no Castle presumption. Castle is not a loophole to allow lethal force to be used in defense of property as the residence or vehicle must be occupied at the time that the trespass occurs, so we are back to defense of life versus defense of property.

Finally, some people are irritated that our version of Castle does not explicitly do away with the duty to retreat. This was by design, and believe me, those opposed to Castle attempted numerous times to get the presumption to apply to one single element of the self-defense case only, such as the duty to retreat being eliminated or there being a presumption that "reasonable grounds" exist. The problem with this approach is two-fold. First, it would still leave the actor with the burden of proving ALL OF THE REMAINING ELEMENTS OF THE SELF-DEFENSE case. For instance, if the duty to retreat were eliminated, the actor would still face proving they did not create, escalate or prolong the situation and that there were reasonable grounds to believe and an honest belief that there was imminent danger of serious physical harm or death.

Second, self-defense is court defined as to the elements, and tomorrow the courts could come up with a fourth or fifth element for an actor to prove. Ohio's version of Castle avoids all of these pitfalls by making the Castle presumption apply AS TO THE ENTIRE ACT OF SELF-DEFENSE, whether it is a 3, 4 or 5 step test. So it includes the elimination of all elements within the test, including the duty to retreat, so long as the presumption applies. This is a far superior approach, making the presumption conclusive as to the entire act rather than one element of the act.

The carrying of a concealed handgun is among the most serious decisions a citizen can make, a decision that comes with great responsibility, and corresponding liability. Aside from the obvious liability involved with shooting another human being, which is largely eliminated in the world of Castle Doctrine and the civil reforms contained therein, there are many other "stealth" liability issues that come with carrying a concealed handgun.

First and foremost, the gun owner is introducing a loaded handgun into everyday society. This comes with an inherent duty to make sure that no unauthorized person gains access to the handgun. Police/law enforcement officers go through rigorous hours of training on gun retention drills. The average CHL is not going to be provided this kind of training. Regardless, the CHL needs to take steps designed to keep a passerby from getting to the handgun. This is a multi-disciplinary approach: is the handgun concealed so that it isn't noticeable to untrained eyes, secured in a holster that has a thumb strap or some other retention device, or is it just tucked in a waistband with an ill-fitting shirt? Most people are shocked to learn just how quick and easy it is to snatch a gun from someone.

Unauthorized access also is an issue with storage or transporting a handgun. There was at least one report of a handgun stolen out of a vehicle from a CHL holder in the first 75 days of Ohio's concealed carry law. Is the gun locked in the car, or is it locked *to* the car with a cable lock? When the CHL gets home, there will probably be a temptation to take the handgun off and set it someplace. Is the handgun set briefly on the kitchen counter, in full access of children, or is the time taken to go the bedroom and lock it up? An even more serious variation of this would be using a public restroom. When nature calls and the pants, and the holster, are moved around the hips, there is going to be the temptation, and maybe the need, to set the handgun someplace. Folks, we can't make these risks up, they are far too strange. So strange you have to know we are telling the truth. Proper care must be taken to prevent unauthorized access, and triple check to make sure it isn't left someplace. Going to the mall to try on some new slacks? Think it is OK to leave the handgun in the dressing room? The variations on this theme are practically endless.

The facts show that the overwhelming majority of accidental discharges from firearms occur while a semi-automatic is being loaded or unloaded. Is this activity occurring in a second story, so that an accidental discharge will pass through the floors below, or maybe outside the house so that the discharge passes into a neighbor's house, or is the handgun being loaded while held over a 5-gallon bucket full of sand? The majority of accidental discharges occur because the trigger is pulled, accidentally. I wrote those words almost 11 years ago. As I finished the Third Edition of this book, someone forwarded me a newspaper story from Utah showing that a licensee blew apart a public toilet when he went to stand up and pull his pants up and the gun fell out of the holster and discharged. Thankfully no one was hurt. As I finished the Fourth Edition of this book, I saw pictures of people with a CHL who shot themselves in the buttocks and legs. They were both hurt. These things have happened and continue to happen. Don't be the next accidental discharge, please.

The prevailing wisdom on ammunition selection is that hand-loaded ammunition should not be carried for self-defense loads. While a competent hand loader will create the most accurate, most reliable load for his handgun, and this should be a desirable result, the overwhelming opinion published in firearm literature is that hand loads should not be used due to "liability concerns." Unfortunately, this has been repeated so often that it has now become accepted as general opinion, and would be used against the hand loader at trial. Further, even as a skeptic and one who shoots 99.9% hand-loads, I have to concede I don't carry hand-loads because I know at any court hearing the only way it will ever be presented is "ordinary bullets weren't deadly enough for this guy." No one is going to believe I went to the time and expense to cook up less-deadly rounds. As for commercial ammunition, any ammunition selection is going to be attacked at trial. There are many resources available on the Internet, and many different types of test results. One published authority recommends carrying what your local police department carries. In the end, what works best for one handgun might not work for another, so make sure to test the alternatives thoroughly.

Several published "authorities" opine that gun owners cannot have trigger work or other gun-smithing done to their carry guns because of "liability." I have yet to have someone present me a plausible scenario of how this creates additional liability. On an accidental discharge and civil liability, sure, maybe you become 105% liable versus 100%. But in any conceivable civil scenario I can envision, you have liability from day one regardless of whether your gun is stock or had a trigger job. It is your responsibility to make sure the gun you carry is mechanically functional and reliable, and if you tinker with it, you might make it less functional or reliable. Honestly, what does that have to do with whether it is your liability from the first moment, even without the tinkering? You drop your gun, that is your accident and your liability. If the gun is a POS and it fires, well, first off, you chose to carry an unsafe POS, so you have liability starting with your equipment selection, and second off, you have liability for dropping the POS. At best, maybe you have a gun manufacturer sitting next to you at the defense table with Plaintiff's counsel arguing the gun wasn't drop-safe out of the box and they shouldn't have marketed the POS. You still chose it and dropped it, so your best case scenario is to shift the civil liability. Worse case, you were already liable, and maybe they try to hang punitive damages on you for stupid modifications, and all of us legal practioners know just how rare punitive damages are.

Stated another way, you are already liable for everything that comes out of the barrel of your gun. If you have a hack-job done on your gun trigger or safety, you have increased the chances that something will come out of your barrel. If the hack job rises to the level of unreasonable risk of harm, then you may incur some new criminal or civil liability. A professional trigger job or a five-pound factory trigger versus an eleven-pound trigger, or disconnecting a magazine safety, really does not create "new" liability. What it might create is "new" potential for an accidental discharge, but that isn't "new" liability. You have always been responsible for accidental discharges.

In the criminal realm, I am really baffled how anyone feels there is increased liability for gunsmith work. If I shoot Johnny Crackhead, I did so deliberately in defense of myself or others. Whether it took four pounds of pressure on the trigger or eleven pounds, whether there was a magazine safety disconnected or not, I'm not claiming I did not mean to shoot him, I'm claiming I meant to shoot the SOB and would do so again in the exact same circumstances.

If I'm going into a criminal trial or civil trial and claiming I had an accident, I'm already hosed – accidents are my fault In a self-defense case, which involves my deliberate act, not an accident, if the prosecutor wants to try and argue about my trigger pull or the aftermarket bits on my gun, I'm going to respond with "So what? I meant to shoot the SOB who was threatening me and my family and I was going to do whatever it took to make sure the gun went off and the threat stopped."

But what about insurance? Double check your policy language, because most liability insurance policies exclude deliberate acts and criminal acts. So there is coverage for dropping the gun and having it accidentally go off in the bad guy's ten ring, but if you act in justified self-defense, that is excluded from average policies as a deliberate or criminal act. As of the writing of this book, the Second Call Defense is making self-defense insurance coverage available through their website, and that is the only source of affordable, quality coverage the author is aware of.

The gun owner has probably spent thousands of dollars buying a hand gun, learning the characteristics of that gun through many range sessions, spending additional range sessions trying out self-defense loads at $17.00 per 20 rounds, going through competency training, and obtaining the concealed carry license. Given this investment, does it make sense to try and save $10.00 on a holster? To save $100.00 on that legal question that really needs to be answered because the gun owner doesn't want to pay for a consultation with an attorney? The gun owner needs to understand the difference between smart money saved and foolish money "saved."

Ohio has a broad exemption for carrying concealed within the four walls of the gun owner's own home. No license or justification is needed. USE THIS! The place to figure out that your handgun pulls down that favorite pair of pants, or that the handgun falls out of a favorite holster when the gun owner leans over or is in the bathroom, is not out in public.

CHAPTER 12. WHAT TO DO AFTER A SHOOTING

In the unfortunate event that someone is involved in a shooting, they need to be prepared to properly deal with the legal aftermath. This begins immediately post-shooting. I am mostly covering this section in a brief checklist format, and setting that checklist right up front, so it can be found quickly in an emergency.

1. Call the Police
2. Clearly state your name, and your phone number
3. Inform the dispatcher that you are a (CHL)(armed homeowner)
4. State that someone attacked you with lethal force, or was about to attack you with lethal force and you had no choice but to stop them (whichever applies)
5. State that you were in fear for your (your family's) life and the only thing you could do to stop the attack was to shoot the attacker in self-defense
6. Request that they dispatch the police and emergency medical services
7. Tell the dispatcher that you are now putting the phone down but won't hang up
8. Put the phone down, regardless of what the dispatcher is saying/asking. Remember a tape recorder is running and will record any comments after this point
9. When the police arrive, if you cannot safely communicate with the police directly, pick the phone back up and communicate via the dispatcher
10. Whether you are talking directly to the police or the dispatcher, identify yourself, where you are, what you are wearing, and similarly identify any other good guys present
11. Whether you are talking directly to the police or the dispatcher, identify any other bad guys are present, or identify that you do not know if any other bad guys are present
12. Follow all of the directions of the police officer on the scene
13. Once the scene is secure, request any medical attention you or your family needs and then state that you cannot discuss the

incident any further until your attorney is present. Make sure any other family member knows to do this, as you personally cannot invoke their right to counsel, they must invoke it

14. Ask that you be allowed to contact your attorney, or have them contact your attorney on your behalf

15. Keep your mouth shut

If a gun owner becomes involved in a shooting, there are several important things to understand. First, in the majority of cases, the shooter is going to be arrested and the case presented to the county grand jury. The average gun owner is a law-abiding member of society, has not been through the process of being charged with a crime, and will probably consider the following information to be offensive: If the gun owner is involved in a shooting, the first, last and only words to the police should be, "I cannot talk to you until I have consulted with my attorney." This statement is not obstructionist, does not imply guilt, and does not make the gun owner anti-law enforcement. Just keep in mind that it is not the job of the police or prosecutor to "clear" the gun owner. While the police and prosecutor do have an underlying duty to do justice, keep in mind that the first job of law enforcement is to document and prosecute crimes. They are under no duty to help you establish your claims of self-defense. Ask any person thoroughly involved with hands-on criminal justice, and he/she will tell you that the majority of criminal cases depend on statements from the accused to obtain a conviction.

A self-defense encounter is going to trigger psychological and physiological reactions. Your heart rate is going to skyrocket (one of my clients had a pulse in the 130s three days post-shooting.) Your sense of time and hearing are going to be distorted. You might have suffered from tunnel vision and not seen things that are obvious after-the-fact. You might be experiencing unavoidable excitement and elation as a result of surviving the encounter, and this would look damning to bystanders. I cannot stress this enough – you are not in a physical condition that makes you competent to give a statement post-shooting. Any mistake now is going to be magnified hundreds of times over 6 months down the road. Keep Your Mouth Shut until your attorney has a chance to visit with you. If the police are trying to bait you with "well if you have nothing to hide you'd talk to us....give me a break guy, this is clearly self defense, just give me the statement so I can wrap up my paperwork and release you etc." Keep Your Mouth Shut. If police interaction continues despite your request for an attorney, you should ask for medical treatment because you aren't feeling right (breathing fast, heart racing, distracted, can't concentrate etc).

Keeping your mouth shut might mean you spend a night or a weekend in jail. That is a small price to pay. Make sure your family, who is not being arrested, knows to keep their mouths shut until they talk to an attorney. Any inconsistency between what they say and what you say later is going to be magnified and harped upon. If you are in jail, do not discuss the situation with your cellmates, who are likely going to sell you out with inaccurate information, hoping that in return the prosecution helps him/her out. Keep Your Mouth Shut.

A final matter that is really a first matter: You need the name and number of a good self-defense attorney and you need to keep that name and number handy. The guy who drafted your will is not necessarily a good or bad choice, but you need to check into it further. Similarly, the so called self-defense plans or concealed carry insurance might be a good or bad choice. You need to do your due diligence research. Has the attorney predominantly practiced criminal law for most of their career? Do they have prior TRIAL EXPERIENCE in murder/ felonious assault/self-defense cases? What is the majority of their practice? I cannot stress this enough, it is not good enough that you have your neighbor's number in your wallet because he just happens to be an attorney. Is your neighbor a criminal attorney with self-defense trial experience? If not, then that neighbor is going to have little idea what to advise in the immediate aftermath of a shooting.

In Ohio, when someone asks about "expungement," they are almost always asking about applying to seal a record. In Ohio, expungement is a juvenile court process, or a special, limited process for persons with a single type of conviction. I don't state this to be snooty, but to stress that these are "terms of art" and have appropriate, and inappropriate, uses.

"Expungement" can mean R.C. 2151.358, which is a juvenile court statute dealing with records already sealed by the juvenile court pursuant to R.C. 2151.356. After September 30, 2011, "expungement" can also mean R.C. 2953.37, which deals specifically, and only, with people who had a concealed carry license and were convicted of improper transportation under the old car carry law, which micromanaged how a person with a CHL could carry a loaded handgun in a car.

"Sealing of a record" refers to R.C. 2953.32, which allows adult first offenders (those with no more than 1 felony conviction, or no more than 2 misdemeanor convictions, or no more than 1 felony and 1 misdemeanor conviction) to get a court order to seal the record of their case. Certain convictions, listed in R.C. 2953.36, are not eligible for sealing.

"Restoration of Firearm rights" refers to an application filed pursuant to R.C. 2923.14, and deals with restoring a person's firearm rights without disturbing the underlying court records.

Do not confuse sealed records with the restoration of civil rights. Someone can be restored to civil rights by a court, i.e., be allowed to own a firearm again, without having the conviction sealed. This is often the case where someone has a conviction that cannot be sealed because of Ohio's limited statute, yet the conviction is not one that would warrant long-term firearm disability. In these instances, the person will seek restoration of rights, as this will remove the firearm disqualification without sealing the records. If a record is sealed under Ohio's statute allowing for the sealing of a criminal conviction, the person is automatically restored to civil rights with regard to the sealed conviction without requiring a separate application for restoration of civil rights. Stated another way, sealing always grants restoration, restoration never grants sealing.

Expungement

I am not going to cover the process of getting a juvenile court record sealed or expunged. Adult expungement in Ohio is limited to R.C. 2953.37. This section of law was added as part of the new law that removes the old restrictions on how a person with a CHL could carry a loaded handgun in a car. The General Assembly realized these restrictions, a poison-pill addition, were a mistake, and removed the restrictions effective September 30, 2011. In addition, recognizing the mistake, the General Assembly established a new, limited procedure, available only to someone 1.) who had a CHL and 2.) was convicted for violating the car carry restrictions that no longer exist. This person may file an application to have the record expunged with the court that convicted them. The fee is $50.00 for court costs. The prosecution gets a chance to object to the application, and the judge will typically have the probation department prepare a brief report on the applicant. If the judge decides to grant this expungement, it operates as a true expungement – the record no longer exists and cannot be examined by anyone. An order granting expungement automatically restores a person to all firearm rights pursuant to R.C. 2953.33. So a person granted an expungement does not need to file a separate application to restore firearm rights. Additionally, as a complete expungement with no exception, the federal government accepts this as a restoration of firearm rights AND an expungement under 18 USC 921(a)(20).

Sealing of a Record

A first offender may apply, pursuant to R.C. 2953.32, to have the record in their case sealed. A first offender is someone with no other criminal convictions. R.C. 2953.31 specifies what constitutes a prior conviction, and includes, for instance, hit-skip accidents. Applicants should carefully review 2953.31(A) to determine if they are a "first offender" for the purposes of this law. Additionally, certain convictions may not be sealed, even if the person is a first offender. The list of the convictions that may not be sealed is set forth in R.C. 2953.36. Applicants should carefully review this section to see if their conviction is among the list of convictions that may not be sealed.

Assuming the person is a first offender and their conviction may be sealed, the person files an application to seal the conviction with the court that convicted them. The fee is $50.00 for court costs. (Note: I am aware of some counties charging more. This is contrary to law, but typically the applicant is not going to force the issue, thus ticking off the court he is applying to.) The prosecution gets a chance to object to the application, and the judge will typically have the probation department prepare a brief report on the applicant. If the judge decides to grant this sealing of the record, it does not operate to truly seal the record – the record still exists and can be examined by a list of 12 different types of persons, as set forth in R.C. 2953.32(D)(1)- (12). An order sealing the record automatically restores a person to all firearm rights pursuant to R.C. 2953.33. The federal government accepts this as a restoration of firearm rights under 18 USC 921(a) (20) but DOES NOT accept it as an "expungement" because the record still exists and a list of people may go examine the sealed record. I point out this technicality because for a while, at least, NICS was not accepting Ohio orders sealing the record because they were considering the orders only in the context of an expungement, instead of considering the order as one that also completely restored firearm rights.

Restoration of Firearm Rights

Effective September 30, 2011, a person who is under firearm disability, and is not eligible for sealing or expungement of the conviction, or, if the disability is one other than for a conviction (i.e. temporarily, but involuntarily, admitted to a mental hospital etc), they can apply to the common pleas court in their county of residence (not the court that convicted them, unless it is one and the same) for an order restoring their firearm rights pursuant to R.C. 2923.14. There is no set court cost for this application, and it is treated like a typical civil filing. The prosecution gets a chance to object to the application, and the judge will typically have the probation department prepare a brief report on the applicant. If the judge decides to grant the restoration of rights, then that is an order that operates to restore all firearm rights. The federal government accepts this as a restoration of firearm rights under 18 USC 921(a)(20).

A CONVICTION FOR DOMESTIC VIOLENCE CANNOT CURRENTLY BE OVERCOME IN OHIO. Sealing the record or applying to a court to have your firearm rights restored will not work. The domestic violence disability is purely a federal disability, and federal law states, at 18 USC 921(a)(33)(B)(ii), that federal law only recognizes an expungement or restoration of rights from a state that imposes a state-level firearm disability for domestic violence convictions. Ohio does not impose a state-level firearm disability for domestic violence, so the federal government does not honor any Ohio court action attempting to restore firearm rights to someone convicted of domestic violence.

Please note, for orders restoring firearm rights issued prior to September 30, 2011, the order was granted under a statute considered defective under federal law. Federal law only recognizes a complete restoration of firearm rights. Prior to September 30, 2011, Ohio's orders were an incomplete restoration of firearm rights, as some rights were not included. Consequently, the federal government ceased honoring those state court orders, and this is what necessitated the change to Ohio law that became effective September 30, 2011. Part of this new law specifies that the "fix" Ohio passed should apply retroactively to any prior order restoring firearm rights. It remains to be seen how this is accepted by the various courts and agencies. Generally, efforts to retroactively rehabilitate things via subsequent amendment are frowned upon by courts.

Unfortunately, as our communities grow, they sprawl. Further, those looking to escape the congestion and general tension of traffic often are looking to "country land" to build their new homes. This often puts these persons into proximity with gun ranges, public and private, that have existed for decades. Similarly, as existing ranges grow older, or new markets are identified, new ranges must be built, and this typically means establishing a range next to people who are not used to having a range next door.

This invariably results in tension between the neighbors, and this also invariably results in some form of legal pressure being brought against the range. It might be the police, it might be the township trustees, it might be city council or it might be a private attorney filing a lawsuit. The exact identity of the opposite party is really immaterial. What matters is that now the range owner is facing legal pressure and must spend money to respond to the pressure. The only alternative is to give up a range that has a bunch of time and money invested into it.

It is not accidental that ranges are facing scrutiny. The Heller and McDonald decisions were crippling blows to anti-gun activists. Reviewing these cases, the antis have realized that attacking firearms head-on is a losing proposition long-term. Instead, they have turned to ancillary attacks, such as attacks on ammunition, gun shows and gun ranges. If they cannot directly target the guns, they will instead work to make the guns much more expensive and inconvenient to acquire and use. In Chicago, for instance, after losing the McDonald decision, Chicago's city council decided "OK, we will license and allow handguns, but you have to have a training certificate from a gun range to get a license. And, by the way, we have banned all gun ranges inside Chicago city limits." Current efforts include pressuring banks and credit card companies to stop servicing gun-related businesses, and pressuring large retailers to stop selling certain types of guns.

Attacking ranges is part of this plan. Starting about three years ago, gun rights attorneys started receiving phone calls from people who own gun ranges. This was too widespread and simultaneous to be coincidental. Fortunately, Ohio has some fairly robust range protection built into various parts of the Revised Code. Unfortunately, this is not a concentrated, organized package of laws, so the legal practitioner is forced to scour the code to put together the various laws into a package addressing the situation, and then must try to educate the public officials and/or judges involved.

R.C. 9.68

R.C. 9.68, also known as Ohio's preemption and open carry statute, plays a small role in range protection. This provision of Ohio law also contains "preemption" of zoning, to a small extent. Local commercial and business zoning cannot single out the commercial sale of firearms and firearm components. So, to the extent a range also has a gun store, R.C. 9.68 specifies that the local commercial, retail and industrial zoning laws regulating location and hours of operation must treat the gun store equally with all other retail businesses, and cannot result in a de facto ban on gun stores.

R.C. 504.04

This section of the Revised Code is the Township Home Rule statute. Unlike municipalities, which derive their home rule authority from the Ohio constitution, townships get their home rule authority via this statute. Specifically EXCLUDED from township authority is the power to "Establish regulations affecting hunting, trapping, fishing, or the possession, use, or sale of firearms." See R.C. 504.04(B)(6). This means townships have no authority to regulate firearms.

R.C. 1533.83, 1533.84 and 1533.85 and OAC 1501:31-29-03

Collectively, these three statutes are referred to as Ohio's range protection statutes. Generally speaking, these statutes establish range standards, and then provide limited immunity to range owners who substantially comply with these range standards. This immunity prohibits civil or criminal enforcement of any ordinances, resolution, regulation or rules on noise or public safety. Also covered is immunity from general civil nuisance lawsuits, by virtue of courts being deprived of the power to grant injunctive relief in response to any civil nuisance lawsuit filed.

The key to invoking these protections is that the range must be compliant with the range standards adopted by Ohio. Ohio has delegated the development of range standards to the Chief of the Division of Wildlife, and these standards are generally referred to as the "chief's rules." The rules are to cover the design, operation and noise level for ranges. When the General Assembly delegated this authority to the chief, it was done with the limitation that the chief's rules could not be more stringent than the NRA Range Source Book. This, as a practical result, means that Ohio's range standards are those set forth in the NRA Range Source Book. So, to invoke these protections, the range must meet the NRA Range Source Book standards.

Assuming the range does substantially meet these standards, then townships, county commissioners, cities and villages cannot enforce noise ordinances against the range, and cannot require more stringent design criteria. If the range does not meet these standards, then noise ordinances and design standards can be enforced. Similarly, if the range meets these standards, their neighbor cannot sue the range for public/private qualified/absolute nuisance.

What constitutes substantial compliance with these standards? Unfortunately, the case law is all over the place. One appellate court twice required the range's neighbors to provide strict proof of non-compliance. Another appellate court accepted what it conceded was non-expert testimony that was flawed from inception, together with innuendo and a clear misreading of the Range Sourcebook. Unfortunately, as this assault against gun ranges does not appear like it is going to end soon, the case law is going to develop further in this area.

Best Practices for a Range Owner

There is no absolute, guaranteed step a range owner can take to invoke these protections. The court is going to look at the NRA Range Source Book extensively. If you have a small, backyard range, you need to understand that these laws are not going to buy you any slack. Your range needs to be designed and operated per the book, or you are going to be shut down. Similarly, if you have a multimillion dollar range that is cutting edge, you need to make sure it is designed and operated per the book. Something as simple, and stupid, as having a map posted and a range briefing for shooters could be the difference between immunity and an injunction shutting you down.

When was the last time your range performed lead remediation and/ or reclamation. There are Federal environmental laws classifying lead as a hazardous substance and if you don't have a lead plan in place AND UTILIZED, these laws can be used by private individuals to shut down your range.

The most common theme in range shutdowns is rounds leaving the range property. Inspect and replace your backstops. Berms settle over time, and what you thought was a 14 foot berm is actually now a 12 foot berm. Are your steel targets being used as designed? Are you collecting the brass that is thrown forward by some guns? Are you limiting the height at which targets can be set?

While it is not cheap, have an architect/engineer who is familiar and experienced with the Range Source Book review your range for compliance. It isn't cheap, but compared to responding to a lawsuit, it is less expensive, guaranteed. The earthwork to reform a berm, raise it and add ricochet arrestors costs money, but not nearly as much money as attorneys. Keeping your range in compliance is just an ordinary cost of doing business. If you aren't taking it seriously, you should expect to be shut down. It WILL happen, it is just a matter of when.

CHAPTER 15. NFA TRUSTS AND LLCS

"NFA" refers to the National Firearms Act, passed by Congress in 1934 to regulate machineguns, sawed-off shotguns and short barrel rifles. NFA was passed in response to gang violence occurring during Prohibition. People will often also refer to the items covered by the NFA as "Class 3" weapons, but the more correct label would be "Title II" weapons. NFA covers full automatic firearms, short barrel rifles and shotguns, suppressors, destructive devices and "any other weapon (AOW)," which is a catch-all category for nasty bits that don't neatly fall into other categories. (Things a like a handgun disguised as a cell phone.) I just refer to the whole lot as "NFA weapons."

The process to legally own NFA weapons is convoluted and expensive, and residents of some states cannot own NFA weapons because their state law separately bans ownership of NFA items. Ohio is a state which allows ownership of NFA items. NFA items are legal to own so long as they are properly registered with BATFE and a $200 tax per item ($5 for an AOW) is paid. This tax payment is reflected by an old-fashioned documentary tax stamp affixed to the ownership papers. Full automatic firearms are a bit of a special case, as the supply of full autos that may be legally owned by non-dealer/non-law enforcement is fixed. This is due to the fact that new registration of full autos was closed in 1986. Thus, while a person may shop for a new suppressor or new short barrel firearm, they may only shop for a full auto that was legally registered prior to the 1986 cut-off.

Your typical NFA acquisition by a non-dealer is going to begin by obtaining a "Form 4," which is the form ATF uses to transfer ownership of an NFA item from a dealer to a non-dealer/non-law enforcement buyer. There are other forms: Form 3 for a tax free transfer to an NFA dealer, Form 5 for tax free transfer to a legal heir at law and/or transfer to a government entity, Form 2 (used by manufacturers), Form 1 (used by manufacturers). However, Form 4 is the document that most owners of NFA items are going to need.

Once the Form 4 is obtained, the purchaser must fill out the form with the typical personal information, list the NFA item being obtained (by description, manufacturer, model, serial number etc), answer the background check questions, obtain a fingerprint card, attach a color photograph AND THEN have the local chief law enforcement officer sign off on the acquisition. At this point the Form 4 is returned to the dealer selling the NFA item, together with the check for the NFA tax. The dealer sends it in to the NFA branch for processing, which takes 4-6 months. Assuming this is accomplished properly, the dealer will receive back the Form 4 from the NFA branch, and transfer the item to you. You must keep a COPY of your Form 4 with the NFA item. You should keep your original Form 4 someplace safe, like a safety deposit box.

If the owner is going to have a permanent change of address, the owner will need to notify the NFA branch of this fact. If the item owned is a full auto, short barrel rifle or shotgun, or a destructive device, and the owner needs to move the items interstate or temporarily export the NFA item, the owner will need to fill out ATF Form 5320.20 to obtain ATF permission for this temporary relocation. Generally speaking, thee NFA item may, for periods of time, travel freely away from the address on the Form 4 until the relocation would be considered a permanent change of address, or the item is going to cross state lines. Suppressors and AOWs do not currently require a 5320.20 to move over state lines.

If you are moving over state lines, you need to verify that it is legal to own these items in the state you are traveling to.

Increasingly, I am receiving calls from persons who wish to form an "NFA Trust." The rationale behind this is that the above process for a Form 4 is largely altered when the buyer is an entity (trust, LLC, company etc). When the purchaser is an entity, no fingerprint card is needed, no color photograph is needed, no sign off by law enforcement is needed and the NFA Branch does not perform a background check on the buyer, since one cannot background check a legal entity. Typically, a person wants to have an entity formed to be the buyer to avoid local law enforcement sign off, as many chief law enforcement officers have a blanket policy of refusing to sign Form 4s. These persons are not persons who typically are dodging a background check, as the penalty for being in possession of an NFA item if you are under legal disability is quite substantial. Rather, in the past, these people had no alternative, due to the policies of an anti-gun chief law enforcement officer.

Ohio now has a "shall sign" law, requiring the county sheriff to sign the chief law enforcement officer certification on a NFA form. The person seeking the signature must fill out the same application form as the CHL, the second, NFA-specific portion of the application, pay the same fee as they would for a CHL (whether 1 form is being signed or 100, it is only 1 fee) and undergo the electronic fingerprinting. If the sheriff does not receive any information indicating the applicant is under firearm disability, the sheriff is required to sign the certification.

Any entity may acquire NFA items, it does not have to be a trust. All entities are treated equally by the NFA Branch, so there is not an advantage gained by one entity over another as far as the NFA Branch is concerned. Entities may authorize persons to possess and use their property at any time. Given that the process and treatment of the entities are equal, people should base their choice of entity entirely upon other factors.

In Ohio, trusts can be a substantial pain to properly administer, and require a trust document to form. The trust document drafting is fairly critical, trusts can be amended, but there are formalities to abide by. I have seen trusts "blow up" and need massive reforma-tion, amending, or they are outright set-aside. When a trust is used as the Form 4 purchaser, a copy of the trust document is sent to the NFA Branch, and they do examine the trust document. Any trust that is a purchaser on a Form 4 is going to be treated as a Grantor Trust by the ATF and the IRS unless the trust is irrevocable (i.e. the person establishing the trust can no longer choose to revoke it.) Ownership of a trust cannot be transferred.

An LLC is easy to form in Ohio, $125 paid to the Ohio Secretary of State, together with a fill-in form that is submitted online. There are no ongoing fees or taxes to keep the LLC in existence. A single member LLC will never be required to file a separate tax return, and instead income is reported (if >$400.00) on Schedule C of the individual's 1040. The person(s) forming the LLC gets to choose how an LLC is taxed (sole proprietorship, partnership, S corp etc) so there is great flexibility. IF there is more than one owner of the LLC, then partnership or corporate tax returns will need to be filed, even if just to show $0.00 in income. The only time an operating agreement is needed is if the LLC includes more than one person, so there is written agreement on valuing the various owners' interests, winding up etc. Ownership of an LLC can be transferred, and the number and interests of the persons owning the LLC can change periodically.

So, considering the ease of creation and maintenance, the single member LLC has a clear advantage over a trust. Considering that ownership in the LLC may change freely, and ownership of the trust cannot change, this also gives an LLC a clear advantage over a trust in situations where multiple people wish to pool together to buy items, even accounting for the fact that a minimal tax return must be filed each year for the LLC. Here is why: when the grantor of a trust dies, no longer wishes to be involved with the trust or wishes to sell an NFA item owned by the trust, this is going to trigger a distribution of the trust assets i.e. a transfer of the ownership of the NFA items previously owned by the trust on to some new person or entity. This will require, at a minimum, the processing of a new Form 5. When the owner of an LLC dies or wishes to otherwise transfer his ownership interest, the asset that transfers is the ownership of the LLC interest, not the ownership of the NFA item. The owner of the NFA item is still the LLC and still via the Form 4. Ownership of the LLC can change without triggering an NFA transfer.

Given that the trust offers no clear benefit over an LLC, and given an LLC has readily apparent advantages with the only downside being that multiple member LLCs must file nominal tax returns, the LLC is almost always the most appropriate and flexible route to creating an entity for NFA purchases.

As a final note, using entities to acquire NFA items has long been considered a loophole around the NFA background check. It is anticipated that some law change will be implemented requiring, at a minimum, a background check of the grantor of a trust or of the owners of an LLC. Given Ohio now has a "shall sign" provision in the law, most people are best served by processing the NFA form in their own, individual name.

Historically, the single biggest impediment to firearm ownership and use in Ohio was municipal ordinances regulating firearms. Townships statutorily have no power to regulate firearms, so we are talking about cities and villages. Given the number of cities in Ohio, there were literally dozens of different laws regulating, in different manners, the exact same firearm conduct. R.C. 9.68 contains statewide "preemption" of all municipal firearm ordinances in the form of a sweeping, affirmative grant of the right to keep and bear firearms. I put "preemption" in quotes because Ohio does not have true "preemption;" rather, what Ohio has a conflicts of law analysis.

The simplest summary of conflicts of laws is as follows: does the municipal criminal law attempt to prohibit that which the state has affirmatively allowed, or does the municipal criminal law attempt to make a misdemeanor offense out of conduct the state already punishes as a felony offense, or does the municipal law attempt to allow what the state already has criminally prohibited. If any of these three conditions exist, there is a conflict of law and the municipal criminal law will not stand.

This is a critical distinction from all prior efforts of the General Assembly to preempt local regulation in other, non-firearm areas. Due to the Home Rule amendment in our Ohio Constitution, the General Assembly may not simply pass a law and say "city you shall not do this" because the Ohio Constitution has already said "city you have the power to do this." "Preemption" means, in the most distilled form of Ohio case law, that the city may not prohibit that which the state affirmatively allows. The state has now affirmatively allowed all firearm conduct unless otherwise prohibited by state or federal law. This "shuts the door" on municipal regulation.

Previously, the cases on Home Rule invariably involved competing levels of prohibitions. For instance, the state prohibits x and y, but the city prohibits x, y and z. This resulted in some legal gymnastics and heavy thinking as the Courts try to determine whether this results in "preemption" of local rule: Does the state not prohibiting "z" automatically equate with the state affirmatively allowing "z," thus preempting the city from trying to prohibit "z?" Unfortunately, the old axiom "that which is not forbidden is allowed" has no home in "preemption" law.

R.C. 9.68 has, for the first time ever in the realm of Ohio "preemption" law, approached this problem of "preemption" by an affirmative, explicit grant of a blanket right to bear arms (i.e. positive regulation) unless otherwise prohibited by federal or state law. Previously, cases like Klein or the recent Baskin case were decided by trying to determine if an ordinance violated an abstract expression of a right in the Constitution, or by trying to determine if the state not prohibiting something via statute equated into the state specifically allowing that action, or most often, the state statute attempting to strip the city of a power granted to the city under the Ohio Constitution via a "city shall not" type of law. These are the methods courts found objectionable when striking down attempts at "preemption" in other areas. R.C. 9.68 avoids these mistakes. The net result is that at some point in time all local ordinances regulating the ownership, possession, purchase, sale, transport, storage and carrying, openly or concealed, of firearms will be invalidated.

It is important to note that the "preemption" provision contains a mandatory attorney fee provision, meaning the municipalities will have to think long and hard about sitting back and waiting to be sued versus taking the initiative, and expense, of going to court against the Attorney General of Ohio. Recently, cities have engaged in a form of brinksmanship where they wait until they are sued and then revoke their illegal ordinance. In such cases, some cities have been successful in arguing that attorney fees can only be awarded if the court ordered them to revoke the ordinance. The city should do the simple thing and revoke their illegal ordinances at the time they are made aware of them

To date, the Ohio Supreme Court upheld R.C. 9.68 in the Clyde and Cleveland cases. Litigation is continuing against Cleveland to determine whether a court can issue an explicit injunction against ordinances on the books, even if Cleveland says they will no longer enforce the ordinances. This is more than a purely academic exercise. Many mail-order companies and convention groups continue to abide by the local ordinances if they are still on the books. These same companies are unwilling to take the risk that Cleveland will suddenly decide to start enforcing their ordinances again. The only insurance against this possibility is an explicit injunction ordering Cleveland not to enforce their laws, or Cleveland revoking their ordinances.

R.C. 504.04

This section of the Revised Code is the Township Home Rule statute. Unlike municipalities, which derive their home rule authority from the Ohio constitution, townships get their home rule authority via this statute. Specifically EXCLUDED from township authority is the power to "Establish regulations affecting hunting, trapping, fishing, or the possession, use, or sale of firearms." See R.C. 504.04(B) (6). This means townships have no authority to regulate firearms.

A final note on preemption: It is important to understand that local ordinances will not cease to exist just because preemption passed and was upheld. Rather, the city must either repeal, or a court must strike down, the ordinance in order for preemption to be carried into legal operation. Until one or the other occurs, the ordinance is still in existence and the unwary gun owner might become a "test case" by virtue of his or her ignorance.

The unfortunate reality for civilian concealed carry is that you, the instructor, will be providing the only formal firearm training that the average citizen will ever receive. Frankly, some of those students should not be given competency certifications. If one of your students ends up committing some blunder, and the authorities start looking back to you, as the instructor of that student, how reasonable is your answer going to be to the questions "How many of your students have you failed? How many have you required to take additional training? Do you keep records to document this?"

Additionally, all good intentions and beliefs notwithstanding, concealed carry training is a business, and the instructor needs to run it as such. Training classes are being advertised all over the place, for wildly varying amounts of money. While it might be tempting to compete on a price point alone, would you rather advertise that your class is the cheapest, or that it is the best value for the money? People are willing to spend money for value. By the time the instructor pays for insurance, class supplies, range time, ammunition, self-employment tax and all other overhead, he will be making less than minimum wage if he is trying to compete on a price point. This is especially true considering that instructing is a second job, and all instruction hours are put in after his regular 40-hour work week.

The one thing that no instructor can do without is A COMPETENT LEGAL PRESENTER. Whether this is an attorney or grizzled police trainer, DO YOURSELF A FAVOR AND SPEND THE TIME AND THE MONEY TO OBTAIN A COMPETENT LEGAL PRESENTATION FOR YOUR CLASS. With the right presenter, this becomes a marketing tool/feature for your class. Ohio's concealed carry law has many pitfalls, and the contents of this book should be considered a bare minimum to completely cover the basics. Additionally, having a legal presenter gives you, the instructor, a two-hour or so break in presenting to your class, and helps keep you fresh and rested.

Another unfortunate reality is that Ohio's passing of concealed carry created a large demand, and many "instructors" popped up to fill this new market. The concealed carry student needs to understand that there are many choices available, and the student needs to be a smart shopper. Price point should be only one of many factors considered. Why is the instructor teaching? How long has the instructor been teaching? Is the curriculum standardized so the student can comparison shop? Are handouts included? Is the instructor affiliated with any gun range? Are references available? IS THERE A COMPETENT LEGAL PRESENTATION GIVEN TO THE CLASS BY SOMEONE KNOWLEDGEABLE? Has that instructor had trouble with competency certifications being accepted? What are the refund/guarantee policies? If the old saying about "only getting what you pay for" is true, have you spent an appropriate amount to prepare yourself for the most serious of personal defense decisions you will ever make?

I look back on the previous four paragraphs nearly 11 years after they were written, and nothing could be more true today. Even in spring of 2015, instructors are cutting corners on training, getting indicted, and their students' CHLs are revoked. While it initially sounds self-serving for me to make those statements, experience has born me out. Overwhelmingly, when a CHL has gotten in trouble, it is because they have gone to a cut rate instructor, such as the one that conducted his range time with Airsoft guns instead of real firearms. If I had a dollar for every time I have heard "my instructor didn't tell me that" when we are talking about the most basic of legal mistakes, my kids would already have their orthodontic braces paid for.

Conclusions

Ohio spent over a decade trying to get a scheme passed to establish a method for the citizen to obtain a predetermination of the legality of carrying a concealed handgun. Ohio's current laws are now mostly consistent with those in the other 48 states with lawful concealed carry. The notable exception is that our training requirement still is quite high, among the top 25% nationwide. Our training requirement combined with the background checks Ohio conducts results in wide acceptance of the Ohio license (39 states as of press time).

Continue to be the law-abiding, model citizen. Powerful editorial boards across the state are against this law, and they are awaiting their poster child. Don't be the one who provides them with their next headline about why citizens cannot be trusted.

If you are not a member of an advocacy group, or if you are and are not actively involved and are not making regular donations beyond basic dues, YOU ARE PART OF THE PROBLEM. No one ever agrees 100% with the policy positions of any group, but nothing helps get bad laws passed more than bickering and infighting among gun owners. The simple truth is that groups have far more clout than individuals when it comes to lobbying, and groups get their clout in direct proportion to the funds they can raise and the members they can mobilize. Writing letters and making phone calls is great, and has a certain effectiveness, but at the end of the day, a well organized group with money to spend makes the difference.

The battle over restaurant carry is a prime example; without the money available to run newspaper ads on short notice targeting Representatives who were waffling, we would still be urging gun owners to write letters and make phone calls to break the impasse and get a vote on restaurant carry. Being able to write this check on short notice is what broke the stalemate, as other Representatives saw the effect of these newspaper ads, and did not want to be treated similarly. Groups only get that way through the volunteer hours and financial support of their members.

Finally, vote with your dollars at businesses that are friendly to your carrying of a concealed handgun. For every business that chooses to ban concealed carry, 3 or 4 alternatives that do not ban are available. Let the business that lost you and the business that gained you know why it happened.

"Under the influence of alcohol" means that a person consumed some alcohol, whether mild or potent, in such a quantity, whether small or great, that it adversely affected and appreciably impaired the person's actions, reactions and mental processes under the circumstances then existing and deprived him of the clearness of intellect and control of himself which he would otherwise have possessed. The question is what effect did any alcohol consumed by the person have on him at the time and place involved. If the consumption so affected the nervous system, brain or muscles of the person so as to impair to an appreciable degree his ability to operate the vehicle, the person was under the influence. **Ohio Jury Instructions 545.25, Sect 6.** "**Appreciable**" means noticeable or perceptible. **O J I 545.25, Sect 7.**

9.68 Right to bear arms - challenge to law.

(A) The individual right to keep and bear arms, being a fundamental individual right that predates the United States Constitution and Ohio Constitution, and being a constitutionally protected right in every part of Ohio, the general assembly finds the need to provide uniform laws throughout the state regulating the ownership, possession, purchase, other acquisition, transport, storage, carrying, sale, or other transfer of firearms, their components, and their ammunition. Except as specifically provided by the United States Constitution, Ohio Constitution, state law, or federal law, a person, without further license, permission, restriction, delay, or process, may own, possess, purchase, sell, transfer, transport, store, or keep any firearm, part of a firearm, its components, and its ammunition.

(B) In addition to any other relief provided, the court shall award costs and reasonable attorney fees to any person, group, or entity that prevails in a challenge to an ordinance, rule, or regulation as being in conflict with this section.

(C) As used in this section:

(1) The possession, transporting, or carrying of firearms, their components, or their ammunition include, but are not limited to, the possession, transporting, or carrying, openly or concealed on a person's person or concealed ready at hand, of firearms, their components, or their ammunition.

(2) "Firearm" has the same meaning as in section 2923.11 of the Revised Code.

(D) This section does not apply to either of the following:

(1) A zoning ordinance that regulates or prohibits the commercial sale of firearms, firearm components, or ammunition for firearms in areas zoned for residential or agricultural uses;

(2) A zoning ordinance that specifies the hours of operation or the geographic areas where the commercial sale of firearms, firearm components, or ammunition for firearms may occur, provided that the zoning ordinance is consistent with zoning ordinances for other retail establishments in the same geographic area and does not result in a de facto prohibition of the commercial sale of firearms, firearm components, or ammunition for firearms in areas zoned for commercial, retail, or industrial uses.

2307.60 Civil action for damages for criminal act.

(A)(1) Anyone injured in person or property by a criminal act has, and may recover full damages in, a civil action unless specifically excepted by law, may recover the costs of maintaining the civil action and attorney's fees if authorized by any provision of the Rules of Civil Procedure or another section of the Revised Code or under the common law of this state, and may recover punitive or exemplary damages if authorized by section 2315.21 or another section of the Revised Code.

(2) A final judgment of a trial court that has not been reversed on appeal or otherwise set aside, nullified, or vacated, entered after

a trial or upon a plea of guilty, but not upon a plea of no contest or the equivalent plea from another jurisdiction, that adjudges an offender guilty of an offense of violence punishable by death or imprisonment in excess of one year, when entered as evidence in any subsequent civil proceeding based on the criminal act, shall preclude the offender from denying in the subsequent civil proceeding any fact essential to sustaining that judgment, unless the offender can demonstrate that extraordinary circumstances prevented the offender from having a full and fair opportunity to litigate the issue in the criminal proceeding or other extraordinary circumstances justify affording the offender an opportunity to relitigate the issue. The offender may introduce evidence of the offender's pending appeal of the final judgment of the trial court, if applicable, and the court may consider that evidence in determining the liability of the offender.

(B)(1) As used in division (B) of this section:

(a) "Tort action" means a civil action for damages for injury, death, or loss to person or property other than a civil action for damages for a breach of contract or another agreement between persons. "Tort action" includes, but is not limited to, a product liability claim, as defined in section 2307.71 of the Revised Code, and an asbestos claim, as defined in section 2307.91 of the Revised Code, an action for wrongful death under Chapter 2125. of the Revised Code, and an action based on derivative claims for relief.

(b) "Residence" has the same meaning as in section 2901.05 of the Revised Code.

(2) Recovery on a claim for relief in a tort action is barred to any person or the person's legal representative if any of the following apply:

(a) The person has been convicted of or has pleaded guilty to a felony, or to a misdemeanor that is an offense of violence, arising out of criminal conduct that was a proximate cause of the injury or loss for which relief is claimed in the tort action.

(b) The person engaged in conduct that, if prosecuted, would constitute a felony, a misdemeanor that is an offense of violence, an attempt to commit a felony, or an attempt to commit a misdemeanor that is an offense of violence and that conduct was a proximate cause of the injury or loss for which relief is claimed in the tort action, regardless of whether the person has been convicted of or pleaded guilty to or has been charged with committing the felony, the misdemeanor, or the attempt to commit the felony or misdemeanor.

(c) The person suffered the injury or loss for which relief is claimed in the tort action as a proximate result of the victim of conduct that, if prosecuted, would constitute a felony, a misdemeanor that is an offense of violence, an attempt to commit a felony, or an attempt to commit a misdemeanor that is an offense of violence acting against the person in self-defense, defense of another, or defense of the victim's residence, regardless of whether the person has been convicted of or pleaded guilty to or has been charged with committing the felony, the misdemeanor, or the attempt to commit the felony or misdemeanor. Division (B)(2)(c) of this section does not apply if the person who suffered the injury or loss, at the time of the victim's act of self-defense, defense of another, or defense of residence, was an innocent bystander who had no connection with the underlying conduct that prompted the victim's exercise of self-defense, defense of another, or defense of residence.

(3) Recovery against a victim of conduct that, if prosecuted, would constitute a felony, a misdemeanor that is an offense of violence, an attempt to commit a felony, or an attempt to commit a misdemeanor that is an offense of violence, on a claim for relief in a tort action is barred to any person or the person's legal representative if conduct the person engaged in against that victim was a proximate cause of the injury or loss for which relief is claimed in the tort action and that conduct, if prosecuted, would constitute a felony, a misdemeanor that is an offense of violence, an attempt to commit a felony, or an attempt to commit a misdemeanor that is an offense of violence, regardless of whether the person has been convicted of or pleaded guilty to or has been charged with committing the felony, the misdemeanor, or the attempt to commit the felony or misdemeanor.

(4) Divisions (B)(1) to (3) of this section do not apply to civil claims based upon alleged intentionally tortious conduct, alleged violations of the United States Constitution, or alleged violations of statutes of the United States pertaining to civil rights. For purposes of division (B)(4) of this section, a person's act of self-defense, defense of another, or defense of the person's residence does not constitute intentionally tortious conduct.

2307.601 No duty to retreat in residence or vehicle.

(A) As used in this section:

(1) "Residence" and "vehicle" have the same meanings as in section 2901.05 of the Revised Code.

(2) "Tort action" has the same meaning as in section 2307.60 of the Revised Code.

(B) For purposes of determining the potential liability of a person in a tort action related to the person's use of force alleged to be in self-defense, defense of another, or defense of the person's residence, if the person lawfully is in that person's residence, the person has no duty to retreat before using force in self-defense, defense of another, or defense of that person's residence, and, if the person lawfully is an occupant of that person's vehicle or lawfully is an occupant in a vehicle owned by an immediate family member of the person, the person has no duty to retreat before using force in self-defense or defense of another.

2901.01 General provisions definitions.

(A) As used in the Revised Code:

(1) "Force" means any violence, compulsion, or constraint physically exerted by any means upon or against a person or thing.

(2) "Deadly force" means any force that carries a substantial risk that it will proximately result in the death of any person.

(3) "Physical harm to persons" means any injury, illness, or other physiological impairment, regardless of its gravity or duration.

(4) "Physical harm to property" means any tangible or intangible damage to property that, in any degree, results in loss to its value or interferes with its use or enjoyment. "Physical harm to property" does not include wear and tear occasioned by normal use.

(5) "Serious physical harm to persons" means any of the following:

(a) Any mental illness or condition of such gravity as would normally require hospitalization or prolonged psychiatric treatment;

(b) Any physical harm that carries a substantial risk of death;

(c) Any physical harm that involves some permanent incapacity, whether partial or total, or that involves some temporary, substantial incapacity;

(d) Any physical harm that involves some permanent disfigurement or that involves some temporary, serious disfigurement;

(e) Any physical harm that involves acute pain of such duration as to result in substantial suffering or that involves any degree of prolonged or intractable pain.

(6) "Serious physical harm to property" means any physical harm to property that does either of the following:

(a) Results in substantial loss to the value of the property or requires a substantial amount of time, effort, or money to repair or replace;

(b) Temporarily prevents the use or enjoyment of the property or substantially interferes with its use or enjoyment for an extended period of time.

(7) "Risk" means a significant possibility, as contrasted with a remote possibility, that a certain result may occur or that certain circumstances may exist.

(8) "Substantial risk" means a strong possibility, as contrasted with a remote or significant possibility, that a certain result may occur or that certain circumstances may exist.

(9) "Offense of violence" means any of the following:

(a) A violation of section 2903.01, 2903.02, 2903.03, 2903.04, 2903.11, 2903.12, 2903.13, 2903.15, 2903.21, 2903.211, 2903.22, 2905.01, 2905.02, 2905.11, 2905.32, 2907.02, 2907.03, 2907.05, 2909.02, 2909.03, 2909.24, 2911.01, 2911.02, 2911.11, 2917.01, 2917.02, 2917.03, 2917.31, 2919.25, 2921.03, 2921.04, 2921.34, or 2923.161, of division (A)(1), (2), or (3) of section 2911.12, or of division (B)(1), (2), (3), or (4) of section 2919.22 of the Revised Code or felonious sexual penetration in violation of former section 2907.12 of the Revised Code;

(b) A violation of an existing or former municipal ordinance or law of this or any other state or the United States, substantially equivalent to any section, division, or offense listed in division (A)(9)(a) of this section;

(c) An offense, other than a traffic offense, under an existing or former municipal ordinance or law of this or any other state or the United States, committed purposely or knowingly, and involving physical harm to persons or a risk of serious physical harm to persons;

(d) A conspiracy or attempt to commit, or complicity in committing, any offense under division (A)(9)(a), (b), or (c) of this section.

…………..

(C) As used in Title XXIX of the Revised Code:

(1) "School safety zone" consists of a school, school building, school premises, school activity, and school bus.

(2) "School," "school building," and "school premises" have the same meanings as in section 2925.01 of the Revised Code.

(3) "School activity" means any activity held under the auspices of a board of education of a city, local, exempted village, joint vocational, or cooperative education school district; a governing authority of a community school established under Chapter 3314. of the Revised Code; a governing board of an educational service center, or the governing body of a school for which the state board of education prescribes minimum standards under section 3301.07 of the Revised Code.

(4) "School bus" has the same meaning as in section 4511.01 of the Revised Code.

2901.05 Burden of proof - reasonable doubt - self-defense.

(A) Every person accused of an offense is presumed innocent until proven guilty beyond a reasonable doubt, and the burden of proof for all elements of the offense is upon the prosecution. The burden of going forward with the evidence of an affirmative defense, and the burden of proof, by a preponderance of the evidence, for an affirmative defense, is upon the accused.

(B)(1) Subject to division (B)(2) of this section, a person is presumed to have acted in self defense or defense of another when using defensive force that is intended or likely to cause death or great bodily harm to another if the person against whom the defensive force is used is in the process of unlawfully and without privilege to do so entering, or has unlawfully and without privilege to do so entered, the residence or vehicle occupied by the person using the defensive force.

(2)(a) The presumption set forth in division (B)(1) of this section does not apply if the person against whom the defensive force is used has a right to be in, or is a lawful resident of, the residence or vehicle.

(b) The presumption set forth in division (B)(1) of this section does not apply if the person who uses the defensive force uses it while in a residence or vehicle and the person is unlawfully, and without privilege to be, in that residence or vehicle.

(3) The presumption set forth in division (B)(1) of this section is a rebuttable presumption and may be rebutted by a preponderance of the evidence.

(C) As part of its charge to the jury in a criminal case, the court shall read the definitions of "reasonable doubt" and "proof beyond a reasonable doubt," contained in division (D) of this section.

(D) As used in this section:

(1) An "affirmative defense" is either of the following:

(a) A defense expressly designated as affirmative;

(b) A defense involving an excuse or justification peculiarly within the knowledge of the accused, on which the accused can fairly be required to adduce supporting evidence.

(2) "Dwelling" means a building or conveyance of any kind that has a roof over it and that is designed to be occupied by people lodging in the building or conveyance at night, regardless of whether the building or conveyance is temporary or permanent or is mobile or immobile. As used in this division, a building or conveyance includes, but is not limited to, an attached porch, and a building or conveyance with a roof over it includes, but is not limited to, a tent.

(3) "Residence" means a dwelling in which a person resides either temporarily or permanently or is visiting as a guest.

(4) "Vehicle" means a conveyance of any kind, whether or not motorized, that is designed to transport people or property.

(E) "Reasonable doubt" is present when the jurors, after they have carefully considered and compared all the evidence, cannot say they are firmly convinced of the truth of the charge. It is a doubt based on reason and common sense. Reasonable doubt is not mere possible doubt, because everything relating to human affairs or depending on moral evidence is open to some possible or imaginary doubt.

"Proof beyond a reasonable doubt" is proof of such character that an ordinary person would be willing to rely and act upon it in the most important of the person's own affairs.

2901.09 No duty to retreat in residence or vehicle.

(A) As used in this section, "residence" and "vehicle" have the same meanings as in section 2901.05 of the Revised Code.

(B) For purposes of any section of the Revised Code that sets forth a criminal offense, a person who lawfully is in that person's residence has no duty to retreat before using force in self-defense, defense of another, or defense of that person's residence, and a person who lawfully is an occupant of that person's vehicle or who lawfully is an occupant in a vehicle owned by an immediate family member of the person has no duty to retreat before using force in self-defense or defense of another.

2923.11 Weapons control definitions.

As used in sections 2923.11 to 2923.24 of the Revised Code:

(A) "Deadly weapon" means any instrument, device, or thing capable of inflicting death, and designed or specially adapted for use as a weapon, or possessed, carried, or used as a weapon.

(B)(1) "Firearm" means any deadly weapon capable of expelling or propelling one or more projectiles by the action of an explosive or combustible propellant. "Firearm" includes an unloaded firearm, and any firearm that is inoperable but that can readily be rendered operable.

(2) When determining whether a firearm is capable of expelling or propelling one or more projectiles by the action of an explosive or combustible propellant, the trier of fact may rely upon circumstantial evidence, including, but not limited to, the representations and actions of the individual exercising control over the firearm.

(C) "Handgun" means any of the following:

(1) Any firearm that has a short stock and is designed to be held and fired by the use of a single hand;

(2) Any combination of parts from which a firearm of a type described in division (C)(1) of this section can be assembled.

(D) "Semi-automatic firearm" means any firearm designed or specially adapted to fire a single cartridge and automatically chamber a succeeding cartridge ready to fire, with a single function of the trigger.

(E) "Automatic firearm" means any firearm designed or specially adapted to fire a succession of cartridges with a single function of the trigger.

(F) "Sawed-off firearm" means a shotgun with a barrel less than eighteen inches long, or a rifle with a barrel less than sixteen inches long, or a shotgun or rifle less than twenty-six inches long overall.

(G) "Zip-gun" means any of the following:

(1) Any firearm of crude and extemporized manufacture;

(2) Any device, including without limitation a starter's pistol, that is not designed as a firearm, but that is specially adapted for use as a firearm;

(3) Any industrial tool, signalling device, or safety device, that is not designed as a firearm, but that as designed is capable of use as such, when possessed, carried, or used as a firearm.

(H) "Explosive device" means any device designed or specially adapted to cause physical harm to persons or property by means of an explosion, and consisting of an explosive substance or agency and a means to detonate it. "Explosive device" includes without limitation any bomb, any explosive demolition device, any blasting cap or detonator containing an explosive charge, and any pressure vessel that has been knowingly tampered with or arranged so as to explode.

(I) "Incendiary device" means any firebomb, and any device designed or specially adapted to cause physical harm to persons or property by means of fire, and consisting of an incendiary substance or agency and a means to ignite it.

(J) "Ballistic knife" means a knife with a detachable blade that is propelled by a spring-operated mechanism.

(K) "Dangerous ordnance" means any of the following, except as provided in division (L) of this section:

(1) Any automatic or sawed-off firearm, zip-gun, or ballistic knife;

(2) Any explosive device or incendiary device;

(3) Nitroglycerin, nitrocellulose, nitrostarch, PETN, cyclonite, TNT, picric acid, and other high explosives; amatol, tritonal, tetrytol, pentolite, pecretol, cyclotol, and other high explosive compositions; plastic explosives; dynamite, blasting gelatin, gelatin dynamite, sensitized ammonium nitrate, liquid-oxygen blasting explosives, blasting powder, and other blasting agents; and any other explosive substance having sufficient brisance or power to be particularly suitable for use as a military explosive, or for use in mining, quarrying, excavating, or demolitions;

(4) Any firearm, rocket launcher, mortar, artillery piece, grenade, mine, bomb, torpedo, or similar weapon, designed and manufactured for military purposes, and the ammunition for that weapon;

(5) Any firearm muffler or suppressor;

(6) Any combination of parts that is intended by the owner for use in converting any firearm or other device into a dangerous ordnance.

(L) "Dangerous ordnance" does not include any of the following:

(1) Any firearm, including a military weapon and the ammunition for that weapon, and regardless of its actual age, that employs a percussion cap or other obsolete ignition system, or that is designed and safe for use only with black powder;

(2) Any pistol, rifle, or shotgun, designed or suitable for sporting purposes, including a military weapon as issued or as modified, and the ammunition for that weapon, unless the firearm is an automatic or sawed-off firearm;

(3) Any cannon or other artillery piece that, regardless of its actual age, is of a type in accepted use prior to 1887, has no mechanical, hydraulic, pneumatic, or other system for absorbing recoil and re-turning the tube into battery without displacing the carriage, and is designed and safe for use only with black powder;

(4) Black powder, priming quills, and percussion caps possessed and lawfully used to fire a cannon of a type defined in division (L)(3) of this section during displays, celebrations, organized matches or shoots, and target practice, and smokeless and black powder, prim-ers, and percussion caps possessed and lawfully used as a propellant or ignition device in small-arms or small-arms ammunition;

(5) Dangerous ordnance that is inoperable or inert and cannot read-ily be rendered operable or activated, and that is kept as a trophy, souvenir, curio, or museum piece.

(6) Any device that is expressly excepted from the definition of a destructive device pursuant to the "Gun Control Act of 1968," 82 Stat. 1213, 18 U.S.C. 921(a)(4), as amended, and regulations issued under that act.

(M) "Explosive" means any chemical compound, mixture, or device, the primary or common purpose of which is to function by explo-sion. "Explosive" includes all materials that have been classified as division 1.1, division 1.2, division 1.3, or division 1.4 explosives by the United States department of transportation in its regulations and includes, but is not limited to, dynamite, black powder, pellet powders, initiating explosives, blasting caps, electric blasting caps, safety fuses, fuse igniters, squibs, cordeau detonant fuses, instan-taneous fuses, and igniter cords and igniters. "Explosive" does not include "fireworks," as defined in section 3743.01 of the Revised Code, or any substance or material otherwise meeting the definition of explosive set forth in this section that is manufactured, sold, possessed, transported, stored, or used in any activity described in section 3743.80 of the Revised Code, provided the activity is conducted in accordance with all applicable laws, rules, and regulations, including, but not limited to, the provisions of section 3743.80 of the Revised Code and the rules of the fire marshal adopted pursuant to section 3737.82 of the Revised Code.

(N)(1) "Concealed handgun license" or "license to carry a concealed handgun" means, subject to division (N)(2) of this section, a license or temporary emergency license to carry a concealed handgun issued under section 2923.125 or 2923.1213 of the Revised Code or a license to carry a concealed handgun issued by another state with which the attorney general has entered into a reciprocity agreement under section 109.69 of the Revised Code.

(2) A reference in any provision of the Revised Code to a concealed handgun license issued under section 2923.125 of the Revised Code or a license to carry a concealed handgun issued under section 2923.125 of the Revised Code means only a license of the type that is specified in that section. A reference in any provision of the Revised Code to a concealed handgun license issued under section 2923.1213 of the Revised Code, a license to carry a concealed handgun issued under section 2923.1213 of the Revised Code, or a license to carry a concealed handgun on a temporary emergency basis means only a license of the type that is specified in section 2923.1213 of the Revised Code. A reference in any provision of the Revised Code to a concealed handgun license issued by another state or a license to carry a concealed handgun issued by another state means only a license issued by another state with which the attorney general has entered into a reciprocity agreement under section 109.69 of the Revised Code.

(O) "Valid concealed handgun license" or "valid license to carry a concealed handgun" means a concealed handgun license that is currently valid, that is not under a suspension under division (A)(1) of section 2923.128 of the Revised Code, under section 2923.1213 of the Revised Code, or under a suspension provision of the state other than this state in which the license was issued, and that has not been revoked under division (B)(1) of section 2923.128 of the Revised Code, under section 2923.1213 of the Revised Code, or under a revocation provision of the state other than this state in which the license was issued.

(P) "Misdemeanor punishable by imprisonment for a term exceeding one year" does not include any of the following:

(1) Any federal or state offense pertaining to antitrust violations, unfair trade practices, restraints of trade, or other similar offenses relating to the regulation of business practices;

(2) Any misdemeanor offense punishable by a term of imprisonment of two years or less.

(Q) "Alien registration number" means the number issued by the United States citizenship and immigration services agency that is located on the alien's permanent resident card and may also be commonly referred to as the "USCIS number" or the "alien number."

2923.12 Carrying concealed weapons.

(A) No person shall knowingly carry or have, concealed on the person's person or concealed ready at hand, any of the following:

(1) A deadly weapon other than a handgun;

(2) A handgun other than a dangerous ordnance;

(3) A dangerous ordnance.

(B) No person who has been issued a concealed handgun license shall do any of the following:

(1) If the person is stopped for a law enforcement purpose and is carrying a concealed handgun, fail to promptly inform any law enforcement officer who approaches the person after the person has been stopped that the person has been issued a concealed handgun license and that the person then is carrying a concealed handgun;

(2) If the person is stopped for a law enforcement purpose and is carrying a concealed handgun, knowingly fail to keep the person's hands in plain sight at any time after any law enforcement officer begins approaching the person while stopped and before the law enforcement officer leaves, unless the failure is pursuant to and in accordance with directions given by a law enforcement officer;

(3) If the person is stopped for a law enforcement purpose, if the person is carrying a concealed handgun, and if the person is approached by any law enforcement officer while stopped, knowingly remove or attempt to remove the loaded handgun from the holster, pocket, or other place in which the person is carrying it, knowingly grasp or hold the loaded handgun, or knowingly have contact with the loaded handgun by touching it with the person's hands or fingers at any time after the law enforcement officer begins approaching and before the law enforcement officer leaves, unless the person removes, attempts to remove, grasps, holds, or has contact with the loaded handgun pursuant to and in accordance with directions given by the law enforcement officer;

(4) If the person is stopped for a law enforcement purpose and is carrying a concealed handgun, knowingly disregard or fail to comply with any lawful order of any law enforcement officer given while the person is stopped, including, but not limited to, a specific order to the person to keep the person's hands in plain sight.

(C)(1) This section does not apply to any of the following:

(a) An officer, agent, or employee of this or any other state or the United States, or to a law enforcement officer, who is authorized to carry concealed weapons or dangerous ordnance or is authorized to carry handguns and is acting within the scope of the officer's, agent's, or employee's duties;

(b) Any person who is employed in this state, who is authorized to carry concealed weapons or dangerous ordnance or is authorized to carry handguns, and who is subject to and in compliance with the requirements of section 109.801 of the Revised Code, unless the appointing authority of the person has expressly specified that the exemption provided in division (C)(1)(b) of this section does not apply to the person;

(c) A person's transportation or storage of a firearm, other than a firearm described in divisions (G) to (M) of section 2923.11 of the Revised Code, in a motor vehicle for any lawful purpose if the firearm is not on the actor's person;

(d) A person's storage or possession of a firearm, other than a firearm described in divisions (G) to (M) of section 2923.11 of the Revised Code, in the actor's own home for any lawful purpose.

(2) Division (A)(2) of this section does not apply to any person who, at the time of the alleged carrying or possession of a handgun, is carrying a valid concealed handgun license, unless the person knowingly is in a place described in division (B) of section 2923.126 of the Revised Code.

(D) It is an affirmative defense to a charge under division (A)(1) of this section of carrying or having control of a weapon other than a handgun and other than a dangerous ordnance that the actor was not otherwise prohibited by law from having the weapon and that any of the following applies:

(1) The weapon was carried or kept ready at hand by the actor for defensive purposes while the actor was engaged in or was going to or from the actor's lawful business or occupation, which business or occupation was of a character or was necessarily carried on in a manner or at a time or place as to render the actor particularly susceptible to criminal attack, such as would justify a prudent person in going armed.

(2) The weapon was carried or kept ready at hand by the actor for defensive purposes while the actor was engaged in a lawful activity and had reasonable cause to fear a criminal attack upon the actor, a member of the actor's family, or the actor's home, such as would justify a prudent person in going armed.

(3) The weapon was carried or kept ready at hand by the actor for any lawful purpose and while in the actor's own home.

(E) No person who is charged with a violation of this section shall be required to obtain a concealed handgun license as a condition for the dismissal of the charge.

(F)(1) Whoever violates this section is guilty of carrying concealed weapons. Except as otherwise provided in this division or division (F)(2) of this section, carrying concealed weapons in violation of division (A) of this section is a misdemeanor of the first degree. Except as otherwise provided in this division or division (F)(2) of this section, if the offender previously has been convicted of a violation of this section or of any offense of violence, if the weapon involved is a firearm that is either loaded or for which the offender has ammunition ready at hand, or if the weapon involved is dangerous ordnance, carrying concealed weapons in violation of division (A) of this section is a felony of the fourth degree. Except as otherwise provided in division (F)(2) of this section, if the offense is committed aboard an aircraft, or with purpose to carry a concealed weapon aboard an aircraft, regardless of the weapon involved, carrying concealed weapons in violation of division (A) of this section is a felony of the third degree.

(2) If a person being arrested for a violation of division (A)(2) of this section promptly produces a valid concealed handgun license, and if at the time of the violation the person was not knowingly in a place described in division (B) of section 2923.126 of the Revised Code, the officer shall not arrest the person for a violation of that division. If the person is not able to promptly produce any concealed handgun license and if the person is not in a place described in that section, the officer may arrest the person for a violation of that division, and the offender shall be punished as follows:

(a) The offender shall be guilty of a minor misdemeanor if both of the following apply:

(i) Within ten days after the arrest, the offender presents a concealed handgun license, which license was valid at the time of the arrest to the law enforcement agency that employs the arresting officer.

(ii) At the time of the arrest, the offender was not knowingly in a place described in division (B) of section 2923.126 of the Revised Code.

(b) The offender shall be guilty of a misdemeanor and shall be fined five hundred dollars if all of the following apply:

(i) The offender previously had been issued a concealed handgun license, and that license expired within the two years immediately preceding the arrest.

(ii) Within forty-five days after the arrest, the offender presents a concealed handgun license to the law enforcement agency that employed the arresting officer, and the offender waives in writing the offender's right to a speedy trial on the charge of the violation that is provided in section 2945.71 of the Revised Code.

(iii) At the time of the commission of the offense, the offender was not knowingly in a place described in division (B) of section 2923.126 of the Revised Code.

(c) If neither division (F)(2)(a) nor (b) of this section applies, the offender shall be punished under division (F)(1) of this section.

(3) Except as otherwise provided in this division, carrying concealed weapons in violation of division (B)(1) of this section is a misdemeanor of the first degree, and, in addition to any other penalty or sanction imposed for a violation of division (B)(1) of this section, the offender's concealed handgun license shall be suspended pursuant to division (A)(2) of section 2923.128 of the Revised Code. If, at the time of the stop of the offender for a law enforcement purpose that was the basis of the violation, any law enforcement officer involved with the stop had actual knowledge that the offender has been issued a concealed handgun license, carrying concealed weapons in violation of division (B)(1) of this section is a minor misdemeanor, and the offender's concealed handgun license shall not be suspended pursuant to division (A)(2) of section 2923.128 of the Revised Code.

(4) Carrying concealed weapons in violation of division (B)(2) or (4) of this section is a misdemeanor of the first degree or, if the offender previously has been convicted of or pleaded guilty to a violation of division (B)(2) or (4) of this section, a felony of the fifth

degree. In addition to any other penalty or sanction imposed for a misdemeanor violation of division (B)(2) or (4) of this section, the offender's concealed handgun license shall be suspended pursuant to division (A)(2) of section 2923.128 of the Revised Code.

(5) Carrying concealed weapons in violation of division (B)(3) of this section is a felony of the fifth degree.

(G) If a law enforcement officer stops a person to question the person regarding a possible violation of this section, for a traffic stop, or for any other law enforcement purpose, if the person surrenders a firearm to the officer, either voluntarily or pursuant to a request or demand of the officer, and if the officer does not charge the person with a violation of this section or arrest the person for any offense, the person is not otherwise prohibited by law from possessing the firearm, and the firearm is not contraband, the officer shall return the firearm to the person at the termination of the stop. If a court orders a law enforcement officer to return a firearm to a person pursuant to the requirement set forth in this division, division (B) of section 2923.163 of the Revised Code applies.

2923.121 Possession of firearm in beer liquor permit premises - prohibition, exceptions.

(A) No person shall possess a firearm in any room in which any person is consuming beer or intoxicating liquor in a premises for which a D permit has been issued under Chapter 4303. of the Revised Code or in an open air arena for which a permit of that nature has been issued.

(B)(1) This section does not apply to any of the following:

(a) An officer, agent, or employee of this or any other state or the United States, or to a law enforcement officer, who is authorized to carry firearms and is acting within the scope of the officer's, agent's, or employee's duties;

(b) Any person who is employed in this state, who is authorized to carry firearms, and who is subject to and in compliance with the requirements of section 109.801 of the Revised Code, unless the appointing authority of the person has expressly specified that the exemption provided in division (B)(1)(b) of this section does not apply to the person;

(c) Any room used for the accommodation of guests of a hotel, as defined in section 4301.01 of the Revised Code;

(d) The principal holder of a D permit issued for a premises or an open air arena under Chapter 4303. of the Revised Code while in the premises or open air arena for which the permit was issued if the principal holder of the D permit also possesses a valid concealed handgun license and as long as the principal holder is not consuming beer or intoxicating liquor or under the influence of alcohol or a drug of abuse, or any agent or employee of that holder who also is a peace officer, as defined in section 2151.3515 of the Revised Code, who is off duty, and who otherwise is authorized to carry firearms while in the course of the officer's official duties and while in the premises or open air arena for which the permit was issued and as long as the agent or employee of that holder is not consuming beer or intoxicating liquor or under the influence of alcohol or a drug of abuse.

(e) Any person who is carrying a valid concealed handgun license, as long as the person is not consuming beer or intoxicating liquor or under the influence of alcohol or a drug of abuse.

(2) This section does not prohibit any person who is a member of a veteran's organization, as defined in section 2915.01 of the Revised Code, from possessing a rifle in any room in any premises owned, leased, or otherwise under the control of the veteran's organization, if the rifle is not loaded with live ammunition and if the person otherwise is not prohibited by law from having the rifle.

(3) This section does not apply to any person possessing or displaying firearms in any room used to exhibit unloaded firearms for sale or trade in a soldiers' memorial established pursuant to Chapter 345. of the Revised Code, in a convention center, or in any other public meeting place, if the person is an exhibitor, trader, purchaser, or

seller of firearms and is not otherwise prohibited by law from possessing, trading, purchasing, or selling the firearms.

(C) It is an affirmative defense to a charge under this section of illegal possession of a firearm in a liquor permit premises that involves the possession of a firearm other than a handgun, that the actor was not otherwise prohibited by law from having the firearm, and that any of the following apply:

(1) The firearm was carried or kept ready at hand by the actor for defensive purposes, while the actor was engaged in or was going to or from the actor's lawful business or occupation, which business or occupation was of such character or was necessarily carried on in such manner or at such a time or place as to render the actor particularly susceptible to criminal attack, such as would justify a prudent person in going armed.

(2) The firearm was carried or kept ready at hand by the actor for defensive purposes, while the actor was engaged in a lawful activity, and had reasonable cause to fear a criminal attack upon the actor or a member of the actor's family, or upon the actor's home, such as would justify a prudent person in going armed.

(D) No person who is charged with a violation of this section shall be required to obtain a concealed handgun license as a condition for the dismissal of the charge.

(E) Whoever violates this section is guilty of illegal possession of a firearm in a liquor permit premises. Except as otherwise provided in this division, illegal possession of a firearm in a liquor permit premises is a felony of the fifth degree. If the offender commits the violation of this section by knowingly carrying or having the firearm concealed on the offender's person or concealed ready at hand, illegal possession of a firearm in a liquor permit premises is a felony of the third degree.

(F) As used in this section, "beer" and "intoxicating liquor" have the same meanings as in section 4301.01 of the Revised Code.

2923.122 Illegal conveyance or possession of deadly weapon or dangerous ordnance or of object indistinguishable from firearm in school safety zone.

(A) No person shall knowingly convey, or attempt to convey, a deadly weapon or dangerous ordnance into a school safety zone.

(B) No person shall knowingly possess a deadly weapon or dangerous ordnance in a school safety zone.

(C) No person shall knowingly possess an object in a school safety zone if both of the following apply:

(1) The object is indistinguishable from a firearm, whether or not the object is capable of being fired.

(2) The person indicates that the person possesses the object and that it is a firearm, or the person knowingly displays or brandishes the object and indicates that it is a firearm.

(D)(1) This section does not apply to any of the following:

(a) An officer, agent, or employee of this or any other state or the United States, or a law enforcement officer, who is authorized to carry deadly weapons or dangerous ordnance and is acting within the scope of the officer's, agent's, or employee's duties, a security officer employed by a board of education or governing body of a school during the time that the security officer is on duty pursuant to that contract of employment, or any other person who has written authorization from the board of education or governing body of a school to convey deadly weapons or dangerous ordnance into a school safety zone or to possess a deadly weapon or dangerous ordnance in a school safety zone and who conveys or possesses the deadly weapon or dangerous ordnance in accordance with that authorization;

(b) Any person who is employed in this state, who is authorized to carry deadly weapons or dangerous ordnance, and who is subject to and in compliance with the requirements of section 109.801 of the Revised Code, unless the appointing authority of the person has expressly specified that the exemption provided in division (D)(1) (b) of this section does not apply to the person.

(2) Division (C) of this section does not apply to premises upon which home schooling is conducted. Division (C) of this section also does not apply to a school administrator, teacher, or employee who possesses an object that is indistinguishable from a firearm for legitimate school purposes during the course of employment, a student who uses an object that is indistinguishable from a firearm under the direction of a school administrator, teacher, or employee, or any other person who with the express prior approval of a school administrator possesses an object that is indistinguishable from a firearm for a legitimate purpose, including the use of the object in a ceremonial activity, a play, reenactment, or other dramatic presentation, or a ROTC activity or another similar use of the object.

(3) This section does not apply to a person who conveys or attempts to convey a handgun into, or possesses a handgun in, a school safety zone if, at the time of that conveyance, attempted conveyance, or possession of the handgun, all of the following apply:

(a) The person does not enter into a school building or onto school premises and is not at a school activity.

(b) The person is carrying a valid concealed handgun license.

(c) The person is in the school safety zone in accordance with 18 U.S.C. 922(q)(2)(B).

(d) The person is not knowingly in a place described in division (B) (1) or (B)(3) to (10) of section 2923.126 of the Revised Code.

(4) This section does not apply to a person who conveys or attempts to convey a handgun into, or possesses a handgun in, a school safety zone if at the time of that conveyance, attempted conveyance, or possession of the handgun all of the following apply:

(a) The person is carrying a valid concealed handgun license.

(b) The person is the driver or passenger in a motor vehicle and is in the school safety zone while immediately in the process of picking up or dropping off a child.

(c) The person is not in violation of section 2923.16 of the Revised Code.

(E)(1) Whoever violates division (A) or (B) of this section is guilty of illegal conveyance or possession of a deadly weapon or dangerous ordnance in a school safety zone. Except as otherwise provided in this division, illegal conveyance or possession of a deadly weapon or dangerous ordnance in a school safety zone is a felony of the fifth degree. If the offender previously has been convicted of a violation of this section, illegal conveyance or possession of a deadly weapon or dangerous ordnance in a school safety zone is a felony of the fourth degree.

(2) Whoever violates division (C) of this section is guilty of illegal possession of an object indistinguishable from a firearm in a school safety zone. Except as otherwise provided in this division, illegal possession of an object indistinguishable from a firearm in a school safety zone is a misdemeanor of the first degree. If the offender previously has been convicted of a violation of this section, illegal possession of an object indistinguishable from a firearm in a school safety zone is a felony of the fifth degree.

(F)(1) In addition to any other penalty imposed upon a person who is convicted of or pleads guilty to a violation of this section and subject to division (F)(2) of this section, if the offender has not attained nineteen years of age, regardless of whether the offender is attending or is enrolled in a school operated by a board of education or for which the state board of education prescribes minimum standards under section 3301.07 of the Revised Code, the court shall impose upon the offender a class four suspension of the offender's probationary driver's license, restricted license, driver's license, commercial driver's license, temporary instruction permit, or probationary commercial driver's license that then is in effect from the range specified in division (A)(4) of section 4510.02 of the Revised Code and shall deny the offender the issuance of any permit or license of that type during the period of the suspension.

If the offender is not a resident of this state, the court shall impose a class four suspension of the nonresident operating privilege of the offender from the range specified in division (A)(4) of section 4510.02 of the Revised Code.

(2) If the offender shows good cause why the court should not suspend one of the types of licenses, permits, or privileges specified in division (F)(1) of this section or deny the issuance of one of the temporary instruction permits specified in that division, the court in its discretion may choose not to impose the suspension, revocation, or denial required in that division.

(G) As used in this section, "object that is indistinguishable from a firearm" means an object made, constructed, or altered so that, to a reasonable person without specialized training in firearms, the object appears to be a firearm.

2923.123 Illegal conveyance of deadly weapon or dangerous ordnance into courthouse - illegal possession or control in courthouse.

(A) No person shall knowingly convey or attempt to convey a deadly weapon or dangerous ordnance into a courthouse or into another building or structure in which a courtroom is located.

(B) No person shall knowingly possess or have under the person's control a deadly weapon or dangerous ordnance in a courthouse or in another building or structure in which a courtroom is located.

(C) This section does not apply to any of the following:

(1) Except as provided in division (E) of this section, a judge of a court of record of this state or a magistrate;

(2) A peace officer, officer of a law enforcement agency, or person who is in either of the following categories:

(a) Except as provided in division (E) of this section, a peace officer, or an officer of a law enforcement agency of another state, a political subdivision of another state, or the United States, who is authorized to carry a deadly weapon or dangerous ordnance, who possesses or has under that individual's control a deadly weapon or dangerous ordnance as a requirement of that individual's duties, and who is acting within the scope of that individual's duties at the time of that possession or control;

(b) Except as provided in division (E) of this section, a person who is employed in this state, who is authorized to carry a deadly weapon or dangerous ordnance, who possesses or has under that individual's control a deadly weapon or dangerous ordnance as a requirement of that person's duties, and who is subject to and in compliance with the requirements of section 109.801 of the Revised Code, unless the appointing authority of the person has expressly specified that the exemption provided in division (C)(2)(b) of this section does not apply to the person.

(3) A person who conveys, attempts to convey, possesses, or has under the person's control a deadly weapon or dangerous ordnance that is to be used as evidence in a pending criminal or civil action or proceeding;

(4) Except as provided in division (E) of this section, a bailiff or deputy bailiff of a court of record of this state who is authorized to carry a firearm pursuant to section 109.77 of the Revised Code, who possesses or has under that individual's control a firearm as a requirement of that individual's duties, and who is acting within the scope of that individual's duties at the time of that possession or control;

(5) Except as provided in division (E) of this section, a prosecutor, or a secret service officer appointed by a county prosecuting attorney, who is authorized to carry a deadly weapon or dangerous ordnance in the performance of the individual's duties, who possesses or has under that individual's control a deadly weapon or dangerous ordnance as a requirement of that individual's duties, and who is acting within the scope of that individual's duties at the time of that possession or control;

(6) Except as provided in division (E) of this section, a person who conveys or attempts to convey a handgun into a courthouse or into another building or structure in which a courtroom is located, who, at the time of the conveyance or attempt, is carrying a valid concealed handgun license, and who transfers possession of the handgun to the officer or officer's designee who has charge of the courthouse or building. The officer shall secure the handgun until the licensee is prepared to leave the premises. The exemption described in this division applies only if the officer who has charge of the courthouse or building provides services of the nature described in this division. An officer who has charge of the courthouse or building is not required to offer services of the nature described in this division.

(D)(1) Whoever violates division (A) of this section is guilty of illegal conveyance of a deadly weapon or dangerous ordnance into a courthouse. Except as otherwise provided in this division, illegal conveyance of a deadly weapon or dangerous ordnance into a courthouse is a felony of the fifth degree. If the offender previously has been convicted of a violation of division (A) or (B) of this section, illegal conveyance of a deadly weapon or dangerous ordnance into a courthouse is a felony of the fourth degree.

(2) Whoever violates division (B) of this section is guilty of illegal possession or control of a deadly weapon or dangerous ordnance in a courthouse. Except as otherwise provided in this division, illegal possession or control of a deadly weapon or dangerous ordnance in a courthouse is a felony of the fifth degree. If the offender previously has been convicted of a violation of division (A) or (B) of this section, illegal possession or control of a deadly weapon or dangerous ordnance in a courthouse is a felony of the fourth degree.

(E) The exemptions described in divisions (C)(1), (2)(a), (2)(b), (4), (5), and (6) of this section do not apply to any judge, magistrate, peace officer, officer of a law enforcement agency, bailiff, deputy bailiff, prosecutor, secret service officer, or other person described in any of those divisions if a rule of superintendence or another type of rule adopted by the supreme court pursuant to Article IV, Ohio

Constitution, or an applicable local rule of court prohibits all persons from conveying or attempting to convey a deadly weapon or dangerous ordnance into a courthouse or into another building or structure in which a courtroom is located or from possessing or having under one's control a deadly weapon or dangerous ordnance in a courthouse or in another building or structure in which a courtroom is located.

(F) As used in this section:

(1) "Magistrate" means an individual who is appointed by a court of record of this state and who has the powers and may perform the functions specified in Civil Rule 53, Criminal Rule 19, or Juvenile Rule 40.

(2) "Peace officer" and "prosecutor" have the same meanings as in section 2935.01 of the Revised Code.

2923.124 Concealed handgun definitions.

As used in sections 2923.124 to 2923.1213 of the Revised Code:

(A) "Application form" means the application form prescribed pursuant to division (A)(1) of section 109.731 of the Revised Code and includes a copy of that form.

(B) "Competency certification" and "competency certificate" mean a document of the type described in division (B)(3) of section 2923.125 of the Revised Code.

(C) "Detention facility" has the same meaning as in section 2921.01 of the Revised Code.

(D) "Licensee" means a person to whom a concealed handgun license has been issued under section 2923.125 of the Revised Code and, except when the context clearly indicates otherwise, includes a person to whom a concealed handgun license on a temporary emergency basis has been issued under section 2923.1213 of the Revised Code and a person to whom a concealed handgun license has been issued by another state.

(E) "License fee" or "license renewal fee" means the fee for a concealed handgun license or the fee to renew that license that is to be paid by an applicant for a license of that type.

(F) "Peace officer" has the same meaning as in section 2935.01 of the Revised Code.

(G) "State correctional institution" has the same meaning as in section 2967.01 of the Revised Code.

(H) "Civil protection order" means a protection order issued, or consent agreement approved, under section 2903.214 or 3113.31 of the Revised Code.

(I) "Temporary protection order" means a protection order issued under section 2903.213 or 2919.26 of the Revised Code.

(J) "Protection order issued by a court of another state" has the same meaning as in section 2919.27 of the Revised Code.

(K) "Child day-care center," "type A family day-care home" and "type B family day-care home" have the same meanings as in section 5104.01 of the Revised Code.

(L) "Foreign air transportation," "interstate air transportation," and "intrastate air transportation" have the same meanings as in 49 U.S.C. 40102, as now or hereafter amended.

(M) "Commercial motor vehicle" has the same meaning as in division (A) of section 4506.25 of the Revised Code.

(N) "Motor carrier enforcement unit" has the same meaning as in section 2923.16 of the Revised Code.

2923.125 Application and licensing process.

It is the intent of the general assembly that Ohio concealed handgun license law be compliant with the national instant criminal background check system, that the bureau of alcohol, tobacco, firearms and explosives is able to determine that Ohio law is compliant with the national instant criminal background check system, and that no person shall be eligible to receive a concealed handgun license permit under section 2923.125 or 2923.1213 of the Revised Code unless the person is eligible lawfully to receive or possess a firearm in the United States.

(A) This section applies with respect to the application for and issuance by this state of concealed handgun licenses other than concealed handgun licenses on a temporary emergency basis that are issued under section 2923.1213 of the Revised Code. Upon the request of a person who wishes to obtain a concealed handgun license with respect to which this section applies or to renew a concealed handgun license with respect to which this section applies, a sheriff, as provided in division (I) of this section, shall provide to the person free of charge an application form and the web site address at which a printable version of the application form that can be downloaded and the pamphlet described in division (B) of section 109.731 of the Revised Code may be found. A sheriff shall accept a completed application form and the fee, items, materials, and information specified in divisions (B)(1) to (5) of this section at the times and in the manners described in division (I) of this section.

(B) An applicant for a concealed handgun license who is a resident of this state shall submit a completed application form and all of the material and information described in divisions (B)(1) to (6) of this section to the sheriff of the county in which the applicant resides or to the sheriff of any county adjacent to the county in which the applicant resides. An applicant for a license who resides in another state shall submit a completed application form and all of the material and information described in divisions (B)(1) to (7) of this section to the sheriff of the county in which the applicant is employed or to the sheriff of any county adjacent to the county in which the applicant is employed:

(1)(a) A nonrefundable license fee as described in either of the following:

(i) For an applicant who has been a resident of this state for five or more years, a fee of sixty-seven dollars;

(ii) For an applicant who has been a resident of this state for less than five years or who is not a resident of this state, but who is employed in this state, a fee of sixty-seven dollars plus the actual cost of having a background check performed by the federal bureau of investigation.

(b) No sheriff shall require an applicant to pay for the cost of a background check performed by the bureau of criminal identification and investigation.

(c) A sheriff shall waive the payment of the license fee described in division (B)(1)(a) of this section in connection with an initial or renewal application for a license that is submitted by an applicant who is a retired peace officer, a retired person described in division (B)(1)(b) of section 109.77 of the Revised Code, or a retired federal law enforcement officer who, prior to retirement, was authorized under federal law to carry a firearm in the course of duty, unless the retired peace officer, person, or federal law enforcement officer retired as the result of a mental disability.

(d) The sheriff shall deposit all fees paid by an applicant under division (B)(1)(a) of this section into the sheriff's concealed handgun license issuance fund established pursuant to section 311.42 of the Revised Code. The county shall distribute the fees in accordance with section 311.42 of the Revised Code.

(2) A color photograph of the applicant that was taken within thirty days prior to the date of the application;

(3) One or more of the following competency certifications, each of which shall reflect that, regarding a certification described in division (B)(3)(a), (b), (c), (e), or (f) of this section, within the three years immediately preceding the application the applicant has performed that to which the competency certification relates and that, regarding a certification described in division (B)(3)(d) of this section, the applicant currently is an active or reserve member of the armed forces of the United States or within the ten years immediately preceding the application the honorable discharge or retirement to which the competency certification relates occurred:

(a) An original or photocopy of a certificate of completion of a firearms safety, training, or requalification or firearms safety instructor course, class, or program that was offered by or under the auspices of a national gun advocacy organization and that complies with the requirements set forth in division (G) of this section;

(b) An original or photocopy of a certificate of completion of a firearms safety, training, or requalification or firearms safety instructor course, class, or program that satisfies all of the following criteria:

(i) It was open to members of the general public.

(ii) It utilized qualified instructors who were certified by a national gun advocacy organization, the executive director of the Ohio peace officer training commission pursuant to section 109.75 or 109.78 of the Revised Code, or a governmental official or entity of another state.

(iii) It was offered by or under the auspices of a law enforcement agency of this or another state or the United States, a public or private college, university, or other similar postsecondary educational institution located in this or another state, a firearms training school located in this or another state, or another type of public or private entity or organization located in this or another state.

(iv) It complies with the requirements set forth in division (G) of this section.

(c) An original or photocopy of a certificate of completion of a state, county, municipal, or department of natural resources peace officer training school that is approved by the executive director of the Ohio peace officer training commission pursuant to section 109.75 of the Revised Code and that complies with the requirements set forth in division (G) of this section, or the applicant has satisfactorily completed and been issued a certificate of completion of a basic firearms training program, a firearms requalification training program, or another basic training program described in section 109.78 or 109.801

of the Revised Code that complies with the requirements set forth in division (G) of this section;

(d) A document that evidences both of the following:

(i) That the applicant is an active or reserve member of the armed forces of the United States, has retired from or was honorably discharged from military service in the active or reserve armed forces of the United States, is a retired trooper of the state highway patrol, or is a retired peace officer or federal law enforcement officer described in division (B)(1) of this section or a retired person described in division (B)(1)(b) of section 109.77 of the Revised Code and division (B)(1) of this section;

(ii) That, through participation in the military service or through the former employment described in division (B)(3)(d)(i) of this section, the applicant acquired experience with handling handguns or other firearms, and the experience so acquired was equivalent to training that the applicant could have acquired in a course, class, or program described in division (B)(3)(a), (b), or (c) of this section.

(e) A certificate or another similar document that evidences satisfactory completion of a firearms training, safety, or requalification or firearms safety instructor course, class, or program that is not otherwise described in division (B)(3)(a), (b), (c), or (d) of this section, that was conducted by an instructor who was certified by an official or entity of the government of this or another state or the United States or by a national gun advocacy organization, and that complies with the requirements set forth in division (G) of this section;

(f) An affidavit that attests to the applicant's satisfactory completion of a course, class, or program described in division (B)(3)(a), (b), (c), or (e) of this section and that is subscribed by the applicant's instructor or an authorized representative of the entity that offered the course, class, or program or under whose auspices the course, class, or program was offered;

(g) A document that evidences that the applicant has successfully completed the Ohio peace officer training program described in section 109.79 of the Revised Code.

(4) A certification by the applicant that the applicant has read the pamphlet prepared by the Ohio peace officer training commission pursuant to section 109.731 of the Revised Code that reviews firearms, dispute resolution, and use of deadly force matters.

(5) A set of fingerprints of the applicant provided as described in section 311.41 of the Revised Code through use of an electronic fingerprint reading device or, if the sheriff to whom the application is submitted does not possess and does not have ready access to the use of such a reading device, on a standard impression sheet prescribed pursuant to division (C)(2) of section 109.572 of the Revised Code.

(6) If the applicant is not a citizen or national of the United States, the name of the applicant's country of citizenship and the applicant's alien registration number issued by the United States citizenship and immigration services agency.

(7) If the applicant resides in another state, adequate proof of employment in Ohio.

(C) Upon receipt of the completed application form, supporting documentation, and, if not waived, license fee of an applicant under this section, a sheriff, in the manner specified in section 311.41 of the Revised Code, shall conduct or cause to be conducted the criminal records check and the incompetency records check described in section 311.41 of the Revised Code.

(D)(1) Except as provided in division (D)(3) of this section, within forty-five days after a sheriff's receipt of an applicant's completed application form for a concealed handgun license under this section, the supporting documentation, and, if not waived, the license fee, the sheriff shall make available through the law enforcement automated data system in accordance with division (H) of this section the information described in that division and, upon making the information available through the system, shall issue to the applicant a concealed handgun license that shall expire as described in division (D)(2)(a) of this section if all of the following apply:

(a) The applicant is legally living in the United States. For purposes of division (D)(1)(a) of this section, if a person is absent from the United States in compliance with military or naval orders as an active or reserve member of the armed forces of the United States and if prior to leaving the United States the person was legally living in the United States, the person, solely by reason of that absence, shall not be considered to have lost the person's status as living in the United States.

(b) The applicant is at least twenty-one years of age.

(c) The applicant is not a fugitive from justice.

(d) The applicant is not under indictment for or otherwise charged with a felony; an offense under Chapter 2925., 3719., or 4729. of the Revised Code that involves the illegal possession, use, sale, administration, or distribution of or trafficking in a drug of abuse; a misdemeanor offense of violence; or a violation of section 2903.14 or 2923.1211 of the Revised Code.

(e) Except as otherwise provided in division (D)(4) or (5) of this section, the applicant has not been convicted of or pleaded guilty to a felony or an offense under Chapter 2925., 3719., or 4729. of the Revised Code that involves the illegal possession, use, sale, administration, or distribution of or trafficking in a drug of abuse; has not been adjudicated a delinquent child for committing an act that if committed by an adult would be a felony or would be an offense under Chapter 2925., 3719., or 4729. of the Revised Code that involves the illegal possession, use, sale, administration, or distribution of or trafficking in a drug of abuse; has not been convicted of, pleaded guilty to, or adjudicated a delinquent child for committing a violation of section 2903.13 of the Revised Code when the victim of the violation is a peace officer, regardless of whether the applicant was sentenced under division (C)(4) of that section; and has not been convicted of, pleaded guilty to, or adjudicated a delinquent child for committing any other offense that is not previously described in this division that is a misdemeanor punishable by imprisonment for a term exceeding one year.

(f) Except as otherwise provided in division (D)(4) or (5) of this section, the applicant, within three years of the date of the application, has not been convicted of or pleaded guilty to a misdemeanor offense of violence other than a misdemeanor violation of section 2921.33 of the Revised Code or a violation of section 2903.13 of the Revised Code when the victim of the violation is a peace officer, or a misdemeanor violation of section 2923.1211 of the Revised Code; and has not been adjudicated a delinquent child for committing an act that if committed by an adult would be a misdemeanor offense of violence other than a misdemeanor violation of section 2921.33 of the Revised Code or a violation of section 2903.13 of the Revised Code when the victim of the violation is a peace officer or for committing an act that if committed by an adult would be a misdemeanor violation of section 2923.1211 of the Revised Code.

(g) Except as otherwise provided in division (D)(1)(e) of this section, the applicant, within five years of the date of the application, has not been convicted of, pleaded guilty to, or adjudicated a delinquent child for committing two or more violations of section 2903.13 or 2903.14 of the Revised Code.

(h) Except as otherwise provided in division (D)(4) or (5) of this section, the applicant, within ten years of the date of the application, has not been convicted of, pleaded guilty to, or adjudicated a delinquent child for committing a violation of section 2921.33 of the Revised Code.

(i) The applicant has not been adjudicated as a mental defective, has not been committed to any mental institution, is not under adjudication of mental incompetence, has not been found by a court to be a mentally ill person subject to court order, and is not an involuntary patient other than one who is a patient only for purposes of observation. As used in this division, "mentally ill person subject to court order" and "patient" have the same meanings as in section 5122.01 of the Revised Code.

(j) The applicant is not currently subject to a civil protection order, a temporary protection order, or a protection order issued by a court of another state.

(k) The applicant certifies that the applicant desires a legal means to carry a concealed handgun for defense of the applicant or a member of the applicant's family while engaged in lawful activity.

(l) The applicant submits a competency certification of the type described in division (B)(3) of this section and submits a certification of the type described in division (B)(4) of this section regarding the applicant's reading of the pamphlet prepared by the Ohio peace officer training commission pursuant to section 109.731 of the Revised Code.

(m) The applicant currently is not subject to a suspension imposed under division (A)(2) of section 2923.128 of the Revised Code of a concealed handgun license that previously was issued to the applicant under this section or section 2923.1213 of the Revised Code or a similar suspension imposed by another state regarding a concealed handgun license issued by that state.

(n) If the applicant resides in another state, the applicant is employed in this state.

(o) The applicant certifies that the applicant is not an unlawful user of or addicted to any controlled substance as defined in 21 U.S.C. 802.

(p) If the applicant is not a United States citizen, the applicant is an alien and has not been admitted to the United States under a nonimmigrant visa, as defined in the "Immigration and Nationality Act," 8 U.S.C. 1101(a)(26).

(q) The applicant has not been discharged from the armed forces of the United States under dishonorable conditions.

(r) The applicant certifies that the applicant has not renounced the applicant's United States citizenship, if applicable.

(s) The applicant has not been convicted of, pleaded guilty to, or adjudicated a delinquent child for committing a violation of section 2919.25 of the Revised Code or a similar violation in another state.

(2)(a) A concealed handgun license that a sheriff issues under division (D)(1) of this section shall expire five years after the date of issuance.

If a sheriff issues a license under this section, the sheriff shall place on the license a unique combination of letters and numbers identifying the license in accordance with the procedure prescribed by the Ohio peace officer training commission pursuant to section 109.731 of the Revised Code.

(b) If a sheriff denies an application under this section because the applicant does not satisfy the criteria described in division (D)(1) of this section, the sheriff shall specify the grounds for the denial in a written notice to the applicant. The applicant may appeal the denial pursuant to section 119.12 of the Revised Code in the county served by the sheriff who denied the application. If the denial was as a result of the criminal records check conducted pursuant to section 311.41 of the Revised Code and if, pursuant to section 2923.127 of the Revised Code, the applicant challenges the criminal records check results using the appropriate challenge and review procedure specified in that section, the time for filing the appeal pursuant to section 119.12 of the Revised Code and this division is tolled during the pendency of the request or the challenge and review.

(c) If the court in an appeal under section 119.12 of the Revised Code and division (D)(2)(b) of this section enters a judgment sustaining the sheriff's refusal to grant to the applicant a concealed handgun license, the applicant may file a new application beginning one year after the judgment is entered. If the court enters a judgment in favor of the applicant, that judgment shall not restrict the authority of a sheriff to suspend or revoke the license pursuant to section

2923.128 or 2923.1213 of the Revised Code or to refuse to renew the license for any proper cause that may occur after the date the judgment is entered. In the appeal, the court shall have full power to dispose of all costs.

(3) If the sheriff with whom an application for a concealed handgun license was filed under this section becomes aware that the applicant has been arrested for or otherwise charged with an offense that would disqualify the applicant from holding the license, the sheriff shall suspend the processing of the application until the disposition of the case arising from the arrest or charge.

(4)If an applicant has been convicted of or pleaded guilty to an offense identified in division (D)(1)(e), (f), or (h) of this section or has been adjudicated a delinquent child for committing an act or violation identified in any of those divisions, and if a court has ordered the sealing or expungement of the records of that conviction, guilty plea, or adjudication pursuant to sections 2151.355 to 2151.358, sections 2953.31 to 2953.36, or section 2953.37 of the Revised Code or the applicant has been relieved under operation of law or legal process from the disability imposed pursuant to section 2923.13 of the Revised Code relative to that conviction, guilty plea, or adjudication, the sheriff with whom the application was submitted shall not consider the conviction, guilty plea, or adjudication in making a determination under division (D)(1) or (F) of this section or, in relation to an application for a concealed handgun license on a temporary emergency basis submitted under section 2923.1213 of the Revised Code, in making a determination under division (B)(2) of that section.

(5) If an applicant has been convicted of or pleaded guilty to a minor misdemeanor offense or has been adjudicated a delinquent child for committing an act or violation that is a minor misdemeanor offense, the sheriff with whom the application was submitted shall not consider the conviction, guilty plea, or adjudication in making a determination under division (D)(1) or (F) of this section or, in relation to an application for a concealed handgun license on a temporary basis submitted under section 2923.1213 of the Revised Code, in making a determination under division (B)(2) of that section.

(E) If a concealed handgun license issued under this section is lost or is destroyed, the licensee may obtain from the sheriff who issued that license a duplicate license upon the payment of a fee of fifteen dollars and the submission of an affidavit attesting to the loss or destruction of the license. The sheriff, in accordance with the procedures prescribed in section 109.731 of the Revised Code, shall place on the replacement license a combination of identifying numbers different from the combination on the license that is being replaced.

(F)(1)(a) Except as provided in division (F)(1)(b) of this section, a licensee who wishes to renew a concealed handgun license issued under this section shall do so not earlier than ninety days before the expiration date of the license or at any time after the expiration date of the license by filing with the sheriff of the county in which the applicant resides or with the sheriff of an adjacent county, or in the case of a applicant who resides in another state with the sheriff of the county that issued the applicant's previous concealed handgun license an application for renewal of the license obtained pursuant to division (D) of this section, a certification by the applicant that, subsequent to the issuance of the license, the applicant has reread the pamphlet prepared by the Ohio peace officer training commission pursuant to section 109.731 of the Revised Code that reviews firearms, dispute resolution, and use of deadly force matters, and a nonrefundable license renewal fee in an amount determined pursuant to division (F)(4) of this section unless the fee is waived.

(b) A person on active duty in the armed forces of the United States or in service with the peace corps, volunteers in service to America, or the foreign service of the United States is exempt from the license requirements of this section for the period of the person's active duty or service and for six months thereafter, provided the person was a licensee under this section at the time the person commenced the person's active duty or service or had obtained a license while on active duty or service. The spouse or a dependent of any such person on active duty or in service also is exempt from the license requirements of this section for the period of the person's active duty or service and for six months thereafter, provided the spouse or dependent was a licensee under this section at the time the person commenced the active duty or service or had obtained a license while the person was on active duty or service, and provided further that the person's active duty or service resulted in the spouse or dependent relocating outside of this state during the period of the active duty or service. This division does not prevent such a person or the person's spouse or dependent from making an application for the renewal of a concealed handgun license during the period of the person's active duty or service.

(2) A sheriff shall accept a completed renewal application, the license renewal fee, and the information specified in division (F)(1) of this section at the times and in the manners described in division (I) of this section. Upon receipt of a completed renewal application, of certification that the applicant has reread the specified pamphlet prepared by the Ohio peace officer training commission, and of a license renewal fee unless the fee is waived, a sheriff, in the manner specified in section 311.41 of the Revised Code shall conduct or cause to be conducted the criminal records check and the incompetency records check described in section 311.41 of the Revised Code. The sheriff shall renew the license if the sheriff determines that the applicant continues to satisfy the requirements described in division (D)(1) of this section, except that the applicant is not required to meet the requirements of division (D)(1)(l) of this section. A renewed license shall expire five years after the date of issuance. A renewed license is subject to division (E) of this section and sections 2923.126 and 2923.128 of the Revised Code. A sheriff shall comply with divisions (D)(2) and (3) of this section when the circumstances described in those divisions apply to a requested license renewal. If a sheriff denies the renewal of a concealed handgun license, the applicant may appeal the denial, or challenge the criminal record check results that were the basis of the denial if applicable, in the same manner as specified in division (D)(2)(b) of this section and in section 2923.127 of the Revised Code, regarding the denial of a license under this section.

(3) A renewal application submitted pursuant to division (F) of this section shall only require the licensee to list on the application

form information and matters occurring since the date of the licensee's last application for a license pursuant to division (B) or (F) of this section. A sheriff conducting the criminal records check and the incompetency records check described in section 311.41 of the Revised Code shall conduct the check only from the date of the licensee's last application for a license pursuant to division (B) or (F) of this section through the date of the renewal application submitted pursuant to division (F) of this section.

(4) An applicant for a renewal concealed handgun license under this section shall submit to the sheriff of the county in which the applicant resides or to the sheriff of any county adjacent to the county in which the applicant resides, or in the case of an applicant who resides in another state to the sheriff of the county that issued the applicant's previous concealed handgun license, a nonrefundable license fee as described in either of the following:

(a) For an applicant who has been a resident of this state for five or more years, a fee of fifty dollars;

(b) For an applicant who has been a resident of this state for less than five years or who is not a resident of this state but who is employed in this state, a fee of fifty dollars plus the actual cost of having a background check performed by the federal bureau of investigation.

(5) The concealed handgun license of a licensee who is no longer a resident of this state or no longer employed in this state, as applicable, is valid until the date of expiration on the license, and the licensee is prohibited from renewing the concealed handgun license.

(G)(1) Each course, class, or program described in division (B)(3) (a), (b), (c), or (e) of this section shall provide to each person who takes the course, class, or program the web site address at which the pamphlet prepared by the Ohio peace officer training commission pursuant to section 109.731 of the Revised Code that reviews firearms, dispute resolution, and use of deadly force matters may be found. Each such course, class, or program described in one of those divisions shall include at least eight hours of training in the safe handling and use of a firearm that shall include training, provided as described in division (G)(3) of this section, on all of the following:

(a)The ability to name, explain, and demonstrate the rules for safe handling of a handgun and proper storage practices for handguns and ammunition;

(b) The ability to demonstrate and explain how to handle ammunition in a safe manner;

(c) The ability to demonstrate the knowledge, skills, and attitude necessary to shoot a handgun in a safe manner;

(d) Gun handling training;

(e) A minimum of two hours of in-person training that consists of range time and live-fire training.

(2) To satisfactorily complete the course, class, or program described in division (B)(3)(a), (b), (c), or (e) of this section, the applicant shall pass a competency examination that shall include both of the following:

(a) A written section, provided as described in division (G)(3) of this section, on the ability to name and explain the rules for the safe handling of a handgun and proper storage practices for handguns and ammunition;

(b) An in-person physical demonstration of competence in the use of a handgun and in the rules for safe handling and storage of a handgun and a physical demonstration of the attitude necessary to shoot a handgun in a safe manner.

(3)(a) Except as otherwise provided in this division, the training specified in division (G)(1)(a) of this section shall be provided to the person receiving the training in person by an instructor. If the training specified in division (G)(1)(a) of this section is provided by a course, class, or program described in division (B)(3)(a) of this section, or it is provided by a course, class, or program described in division (B)(3)(b), (c), or (e) of this section and the instructor is a qualified instructor certified by a national gun advocacy organization, the training so specified, other than the training that requires the person receiving the training to demonstrate handling abilities, may be provided online or as a combination of in-person and online training, as long as the online training includes an interactive component that regularly engages the person.

(b) Except as otherwise provided in this division, the written section of the competency examination specified in division (G)(2)(a) of this section shall be administered to the person taking the competency examination in person by an instructor. If the training specified in division (G)(1)(a) of this section is provided to the person receiving the training by a course, class, or program described in division (B)(3)(a) of this section, or it is provided by a course, class, or program described in division (B)(3)(b), (c), or (e) of this section and the instructor is a qualified instructor certified by a national gun advocacy organization, the written section of the competency examination specified in division (G)(2)(a) of this section may be administered online, as long as the online training includes an interactive component that regularly engages the person.

(4) The competency certification described in division (B)(3)(a), (b), (c), or (e) of this section shall be dated and shall attest that the course, class, or program the applicant successfully completed met the requirements described in division (G)(1) of this section and that the applicant passed the competency examination described in division (G)(2) of this section.

(H) Upon deciding to issue a concealed handgun license, deciding to issue a replacement concealed handgun license, or deciding to renew a concealed handgun license pursuant to this section, and before actually issuing or renewing the license, the sheriff shall make available through the law enforcement automated data system all information contained on the license. If the license subsequently is suspended under division (A)(1) or (2) of section 2923.128 of the Revised Code, revoked pursuant to division (B)(1) of section

2923.128 of the Revised Code, or lost or destroyed, the sheriff also shall make available through the law enforcement automated data system a notation of that fact. The superintendent of the state highway patrol shall ensure that the law enforcement automated data system is so configured as to permit the transmission through the system of the information specified in this division.

(I) A sheriff shall accept a completed application form or renewal application, and the fee, items, materials, and information specified in divisions (B)(1) to (5) or division (F) of this section, whichever is applicable, and shall provide an application form or renewal application to any person during at least fifteen hours a week and shall provide the web site address at which a printable version of the application form that can be downloaded and the pamphlet described in division (B) of section 109.731 of the Revised Code may be found at any time, upon request. The sheriff shall post notice of the hours during which the sheriff is available to accept or provide the information described in this division.

2923.126 Duties of licensed individual.

(A) A concealed handgun license that is issued under section 2923.125 of the Revised Code shall expire five years after the date of issuance. A licensee who has been issued a license under that section shall be granted a grace period of thirty days after the licensee's license expires during which the licensee's license remains valid. Except as provided in divisions (B) and (C) of this section, a licensee who has been issued a concealed handgun license under section 2923.125 or 2923.1213 of the Revised Code may carry a concealed handgun anywhere in this state if the licensee also carries a valid license and valid identification when the licensee is in actual possession of a concealed handgun. The licensee shall give notice of any change in the licensee's residence address to the sheriff who issued the license within forty-five days after that change.

If a licensee is the driver or an occupant of a motor vehicle that is stopped as the result of a traffic stop or a stop for another law enforcement purpose and if the licensee is transporting or has a loaded handgun in the motor vehicle at that time, the licensee shall promptly inform any law enforcement officer who approaches the vehicle while stopped that the licensee has been issued a concealed handgun license and that the licensee currently possesses or has a loaded handgun; the licensee shall not knowingly disregard or fail to comply with lawful orders of a law enforcement officer given while the motor vehicle is stopped, knowingly fail to remain in the motor vehicle while stopped, or knowingly fail to keep the licensee's hands in plain sight after any law enforcement officer begins approaching the licensee while stopped and before the officer leaves, unless directed otherwise by a law enforcement officer; and the licensee shall not knowingly have contact with the loaded handgun by touching it with the licensee's hands or fingers, in any manner in violation of division (E) of section 2923.16 of the Revised Code, after any law enforcement officer begins approaching the licensee while stopped and before the officer leaves. Additionally, if a licensee is the driver or an occupant of a commercial motor vehicle that is stopped by an employee of the motor carrier enforcement unit for the purposes defined in section 5503.04 of the Revised Code and if the licensee is transporting or has a loaded handgun in the commercial motor vehicle at that time, the licensee shall promptly inform the employee of the unit who approaches the vehicle while stopped that the licensee has been issued a concealed handgun license and that the licensee currently possesses or has a loaded handgun.

If a licensee is stopped for a law enforcement purpose and if the licensee is carrying a concealed handgun at the time the officer approaches, the licensee shall promptly inform any law enforcement officer who approaches the licensee while stopped that the licensee has been issued a concealed handgun license and that the licensee currently is carrying a concealed handgun; the licensee shall not knowingly disregard or fail to comply with lawful orders of a law enforcement officer given while the licensee is stopped or knowingly fail to keep the licensee's hands in plain sight after any law enforcement officer begins approaching the licensee while stopped and before the officer leaves, unless directed otherwise by a law enforcement officer; and the licensee shall not knowingly remove, attempt to remove, grasp, or hold the loaded handgun or knowingly have contact with the loaded handgun by touching it with the licensee's hands or fingers, in any manner in violation of division (B) of section 2923.12 of the Revised Code, after any law enforcement officer begins approaching the licensee while stopped and before the officer leaves.

(B) A valid concealed handgun license does not authorize the licensee to carry a concealed handgun in any manner prohibited under division (B) of section 2923.12 of the Revised Code or in any manner prohibited under section 2923.16 of the Revised Code. A valid license does not authorize the licensee to carry a concealed handgun into any of the following places:

(1) A police station, sheriff's office, or state highway patrol station, premises controlled by the bureau of criminal identification and investigation, a state correctional institution, jail, workhouse, or other detention facility, an airport passenger terminal, or an institution that is maintained, operated, managed, and governed pursuant to division (A) of section 5119.14 of the Revised Code or division (A)(1) of section 5123.03 of the Revised Code;

(2) A school safety zone if the licensee's carrying the concealed handgun is in violation of section 2923.122 of the Revised Code;

(3) A courthouse or another building or structure in which a courtroom is located, in violation of section 2923.123 of the Revised Code;

(4) Any premises or open air arena for which a D permit has been issued under Chapter 4303. of the Revised Code if the licensee's carrying the concealed handgun is in violation of section 2923.121 of the Revised Code;

(5) Any premises owned or leased by any public or private college, university, or other institution of higher education, unless the handgun is in a locked motor vehicle or the licensee is in the immediate process of placing the handgun in a locked motor vehicle;

(6) Any church, synagogue, mosque, or other place of worship, unless the church, synagogue, mosque, or other place of worship posts or permits otherwise;

(7) A child day-care center, a type A family day-care home, or a type B family day-care home, except that this division does not prohibit a licensee who resides in a type A family day-care home or a type B family day-care home from carrying a concealed handgun at any time in any part of the home that is not dedicated or used for day-care purposes, or from carrying a concealed handgun in a part of the home that is dedicated or used for day-care purposes at any time during which no children, other than children of that licensee, are in the home;

(8) An aircraft that is in, or intended for operation in, foreign air transportation, interstate air transportation, intrastate air transportation, or the transportation of mail by aircraft;

(9) Any building that is a government facility of this state or a political subdivision of this state and that is not a building that is used primarily as a shelter, restroom, parking facility for motor vehicles, or rest facility and is not a courthouse or other building or structure in which a courtroom is located that is subject to division (B)(3) of this section;

(10) A place in which federal law prohibits the carrying of handguns.

(C)(1) Nothing in this section shall negate or restrict a rule, policy, or practice of a private employer that is not a private college, university, or other institution of higher education concerning or prohibiting the presence of firearms on the private employer's premises or property, including motor vehicles owned by the private employer. Nothing in this section shall require a private employer of that nature to adopt a rule, policy, or practice concerning or prohibiting the presence of firearms on the private employer's premises or property, including motor vehicles owned by the private employer.

(2)(a) A private employer shall be immune from liability in a civil action for any injury, death, or loss to person or property that allegedly was caused by or related to a licensee bringing a handgun onto the premises or property of the private employer, including motor vehicles owned by the private employer, unless the private employer acted with malicious purpose. A private employer is immune from liability in a civil action for any injury, death, or loss to person or property that allegedly was caused by or related to the private employer's decision to permit a licensee to bring, or prohibit a licensee from bringing, a handgun onto the premises or property of the private employer. As used in this division, "private employer" includes a private college, university, or other institution of higher education.

(b) A political subdivision shall be immune from liability in a civil action, to the extent and in the manner provided in Chapter 2744. of the Revised Code, for any injury, death, or loss to person or property that allegedly was caused by or related to a licensee bringing a handgun onto any premises or property owned, leased, or otherwise under the control of the political subdivision. As used in this division, "political subdivision" has the same meaning as in section 2744.01 of the Revised Code.

(3)(a) Except as provided in division (C)(3)(b) of this section, the owner or person in control of private land or premises, and a private person or entity leasing land or premises owned by the state, the United States, or a political subdivision of the state or the United States, may post a sign in a conspicuous location on that land or on those premises prohibiting persons from carrying firearms or concealed firearms on or onto that land or those premises. Except as otherwise provided in this division, a person who knowingly violates a posted prohibition of that nature is guilty of criminal trespass in violation of division (A)(4) of section 2911.21 of the Revised Code and is guilty of a misdemeanor of the fourth degree. If a person knowingly violates a posted prohibition of that nature and the posted land or premises primarily was a parking lot or other parking facility, the person is not guilty of criminal trespass under section 2911.21 of the Revised Code or under any other criminal law of this state or criminal law, ordinance, or resolution of a political subdivision of this state, and instead is subject only to a civil cause of action for trespass based on the violation.

(b) A landlord may not prohibit or restrict a tenant who is a licensee and who on or after September 9, 2008, enters into a rental agreement with the landlord for the use of residential premises, and the tenant's guest while the tenant is present, from lawfully carrying or possessing a handgun on those residential premises.

(c) As used in division (C)(3) of this section:

(i) "Residential premises" has the same meaning as in section 5321.01 of the Revised Code, except "residential premises" does not include a dwelling unit that is owned or operated by a college or university.

(ii) "Landlord," "tenant," and "rental agreement" have the same meanings as in section 5321.01 of the Revised Code.

(D) A person who holds a valid concealed handgun license issued by another state that is recognized by the attorney general pursuant to a reciprocity agreement entered into pursuant to section 109.69 of the Revised Code or a person who holds a valid concealed handgun license under the circumstances described in division (B) of section 109.69 of the Revised Code has the same right to carry a concealed handgun in this state as a person who was issued a concealed handgun license under section 2923.125 of the Revised Code and is subject to the same restrictions that apply to a person who carries a license issued under that section.

(E) A peace officer has the same right to carry a concealed handgun in this state as a person who was issued a concealed handgun license under section 2923.125 of the Revised Code. For purposes of reciprocity with other states, a peace officer shall be considered to be a licensee in this state.

(F)(1) A qualified retired peace officer who possesses a retired peace officer identification card issued pursuant to division (F)(2) of this section and a valid firearms requalification certification issued pursuant to division (F)(3) of this section has the same right to carry a concealed handgun in this state as a person who was issued a concealed handgun license under section 2923.125 of the Revised Code and is subject to the same restrictions that apply to a person who carries a license issued under that section. For purposes of reciprocity with other states, a qualified retired peace officer who possesses a retired peace officer identification card issued pursuant to division (F)(2) of this section and a valid firearms requalification certification issued pursuant to division (F)(3) of this section shall be considered to be a licensee in this state.

(2)(a) Each public agency of this state or of a political subdivision of this state that is served by one or more peace officers shall issue a retired peace officer identification card to any person who retired from service as a peace officer with that agency, if the issuance is in accordance with the agency's policies and procedures and if the person, with respect to the person's service with that agency, satisfies all of the following:

(i) The person retired in good standing from service as a peace officer with the public agency, and the retirement was not for reasons of mental instability.

(ii) Before retiring from service as a peace officer with that agency, the person was authorized to engage in or supervise the prevention, detection, investigation, or prosecution of, or the incarceration of any person for, any violation of law and the person had statutory powers of arrest.

(iii) At the time of the person's retirement as a peace officer with that agency, the person was trained and qualified to carry firearms in the performance of the peace officer's duties.

(iv) Before retiring from service as a peace officer with that agency, the person was regularly employed as a peace officer for an aggregate of fifteen years or more, or, in the alternative, the person retired from service as a peace officer with that agency, after completing any applicable probationary period of that service, due to a service-connected disability, as determined by the agency.

(b) A retired peace officer identification card issued to a person under division (F)(2)(a) of this section shall identify the person by name, contain a photograph of the person, identify the public agency of this state or of the political subdivision of this state from which the person retired as a peace officer and that is issuing the identification card, and specify that the person retired in good standing from service as a peace officer with the issuing public agency and satisfies the criteria set forth in divisions (F)(2)(a)(i) to (iv) of this section. In addition to the required content specified in this division, a retired peace officer identification card issued to a person under division (F)(2)(a) of this section may include the firearms requalification certification described in division (F)(3) of this section, and if the identification card includes that certification, the identification card shall serve as the firearms requalification certification for the retired peace officer. If the issuing public agency issues credentials to active law enforcement officers who serve the agency, the agency may comply with division (F)(2)(a) of this section by issuing the same credentials to persons who retired from service as a peace officer with the agency and who satisfy the criteria set forth in divisions (F)(2)(a)(i) to (iv) of this section, provided that the credentials so issued to retired peace officers are stamped with the word "RETIRED."

(c) A public agency of this state or of a political subdivision of this state may charge persons who retired from service as a peace officer with the agency a reasonable fee for issuing to the person a retired peace officer identification card pursuant to division (F)(2)(a) of this section.

(3) If a person retired from service as a peace officer with a public agency of this state or of a political subdivision of this state and the person satisfies the criteria set forth in divisions (F)(2)(a)(i) to (iv) of this section, the public agency may provide the retired peace officer with the opportunity to attend a firearms requalification program that is approved for purposes of firearms requalification required under section 109.801 of the Revised Code. The retired peace officer may be required to pay the cost of the course.

If a retired peace officer who satisfies the criteria set forth in divisions (F)(2)(a)(i) to (iv) of this section attends a firearms requalification program that is approved for purposes of firearms requalification required under section 109.801 of the Revised Code, the retired peace officer's successful completion of the firearms requalification program requalifies the retired peace officer for purposes of division (F) of this section for five years from the date on which the program was successfully completed, and the requalification is valid during that five-year period. If a retired peace officer who satisfies the criteria set forth in divisions (F)(2)(a)(i) to (iv) of this section satisfactorily completes such a firearms requalification program, the retired peace officer shall be issued a firearms requalification certification that identifies the retired peace officer by name, identifies the entity that taught the program, specifies that the retired peace officer successfully completed the program, specifies the date on which the course was successfully completed, and specifies that the requalification is valid for five years from that date of successful completion. The firearms requalification certification for a retired peace officer may be included in the retired peace officer identification card issued to the retired peace officer under division (F)(2) of this section.

A retired peace officer who attends a firearms requalification program that is approved for purposes of firearms requalification required under section 109.801 of the Revised Code may be required to pay the cost of the program.

(G) As used in this section:

(1) "Qualified retired peace officer" means a person who satisfies all of the following:

(a) The person satisfies the criteria set forth in divisions (F)(2)(a)(i) to (v) of this section.

(b) The person is not under the influence of alcohol or another intoxicating or hallucinatory drug or substance.

(c) The person is not prohibited by federal law from receiving firearms.

(2) "Retired peace officer identification card" means an identification card that is issued pursuant to division (F)(2) of this section to a person who is a retired peace officer.

THE OHIO GUIDE TO FIREARM LAWS

(3) "Government facility of this state or a political subdivision of this state" means any of the following:

(a) A building or part of a building that is owned or leased by the government of this state or a political subdivision of this state and where employees of the government of this state or the political subdivision regularly are present for the purpose of performing their official duties as employees of the state or political subdivision;

(b) The office of a deputy registrar serving pursuant to Chapter 4503. of the Revised Code that is used to perform deputy registrar functions.

2923.127 Challenging denial of license.

(A) If a sheriff denies an application for a concealed handgun license under section 2923.125 of the Revised Code, denies the renewal of a concealed handgun license under that section, or denies an application for a concealed handgun license on a temporary emergency basis under section 2923.1213 of the Revised Code as a result of the criminal records check conducted pursuant to section 311.41 of the Revised Code and if the applicant believes the denial was based on incorrect information reported by the source the sheriff used in conducting the criminal records check, the applicant may challenge the criminal records check results using whichever of the following is applicable:

(1) If the bureau of criminal identification and investigation performed the criminal records check, by using the bureau's existing challenge and review procedures;

(2) If division (A)(1) of this section does not apply, by using the existing challenge and review procedure of the sheriff who denied the application or, if the sheriff does not have a challenge and review procedure, by using the challenge and review procedure prescribed by the bureau of criminal identification and investigation pursuant to division (B) of this section.

(B) The bureau of criminal identification and investigation shall prescribe a challenge and review procedure for applicants to use to challenge criminal records checks under division (A)(2) of this section in counties in which the sheriff with whom an application of a type described in division (A) of this section was filed or submitted does not have an existing challenge and review procedure.

2923.128 Suspension and revocation of license.

(A)(1)(a) If a licensee holding a valid concealed handgun license is arrested for or otherwise charged with an offense described in division (D)(1)(d) of section 2923.125 of the Revised Code or with a violation of section 2923.15 of the Revised Code or becomes subject to a temporary protection order or to a protection order issued by a court of another state that is substantially equivalent to a temporary protection order, the sheriff who issued the license shall suspend it and shall comply with division (A)(3) of this section upon becoming aware of the arrest, charge, or protection order. Upon suspending the license, the sheriff also shall comply with division (H) of section 2923.125 of the Revised Code.

(b) A suspension under division (A)(1)(a) of this section shall be considered as beginning on the date that the licensee is arrested for or otherwise charged with an offense described in that division or on the date the appropriate court issued the protection order described in that division, irrespective of when the sheriff notifies the licensee under division (A)(3) of this section. The suspension shall end on the date on which the charges are dismissed or the licensee is found not guilty of the offense described in division (A)(1)(a) of this section or, subject to division (B) of this section, on the date the appropriate court terminates the protection order described in that division. If the suspension so ends, the sheriff shall return the license or temporary emergency license to the licensee.

(2)(a) If a licensee holding a valid concealed handgun license is convicted of or pleads guilty to a misdemeanor violation of division (B) (1), (2), or (4) of section 2923.12 of the Revised Code or of division (E)(1), (2), (3), or (5) of section 2923.16 of the Revised Code, except as provided in division (A)(2)(c) of this section and subject to division (C) of this section, the sheriff who issued the license shall suspend it and shall comply with division (A)(3) of this section upon becoming aware of the conviction or guilty plea. Upon suspending the license, the sheriff also shall comply with division (H) of section 2923.125 of the Revised Code.

(b) A suspension under division (A)(2)(a) of this section shall be considered as beginning on the date that the licensee is convicted of or pleads guilty to the offense described in that division, irrespective of when the sheriff notifies the licensee under division (A)(3) of this section. If the suspension is imposed for a misdemeanor violation of division (B)(1) or (2) of section 2923.12 of the Revised Code or of division (E)(1), (2), or (3) of section 2923.16 of the Revised Code, it shall end on the date that is one year after the date that the licensee is convicted of or pleads guilty to that violation. If the suspension is imposed for a misdemeanor violation of division (B)(4) of section 2923.12 of the Revised Code or of division (E)(5) of section 2923.16 of the Revised Code, it shall end on the date that is two years after the date that the licensee is convicted of or pleads guilty to that violation. If the licensee's license was issued under section 2923.125 of the Revised Code and the license remains valid after the suspension ends as described in this division, when the suspension ends, the sheriff shall return the license to the licensee. If the licensee's license was issued under section 2923.125 of the Revised Code and the license expires before the suspension ends as described in this division, or if the licensee's license was issued under section 2923.1213 of the Revised Code, the licensee is not eligible to apply for a new license under section 2923.125 or 2923.1213 of the Revised Code or to renew the license under section 2923.125 of the Revised Code until after the suspension ends as described in this division.

(c) The license of a licensee who is convicted of or pleads guilty to a violation of division (B)(1) of section 2923.12 or division (E)(1) or (2) of section 2923.16 of the Revised Code shall not be suspended pursuant to division (A)(2)(a) of this section if, at the time of the stop of the licensee for a law enforcement purpose, for a traffic stop, or for a purpose defined in section 5503.34 of the Revised Code that was the basis of the violation, any law enforcement officer involved with the stop or the employee of the motor carrier enforcement unit who made the stop had actual knowledge of the licensee's status as a licensee.

(3) Upon becoming aware of an arrest, charge, or protection order described in division (A)(1)(a) of this section with respect to a licensee who was issued a concealed handgun license, or a conviction of or plea of guilty to a misdemeanor offense described in division (A)(2)(a) of this section with respect to a licensee who was issued a concealed handgun license and with respect to which division (A)(2)(c) of this section does not apply, subject to division (C) of this section, the sheriff who issued the licensee's license shall notify the licensee, by certified mail, return receipt requested, at the licensee's last known residence address that the license has been suspended and that the licensee is required to surrender the license at the sheriff's office within ten days of the date on which the notice was mailed. If the suspension is pursuant to division (A) (2) of this section, the notice shall identify the date on which the suspension ends.

(B)(1) A sheriff who issues a concealed handgun license to a licensee shall revoke the license in accordance with division (B)(2) of this section upon becoming aware that the licensee satisfies any of the following:

(a) The licensee is under twenty-one years of age.

(b) Subject to division (C) of this section, at the time of the issuance of the license, the licensee did not satisfy the eligibility requirements of division (D)(1)(c), (d), (e), (f), (g), or (h) of section 2923.125 of the Revised Code.

(c) Subject to division (C) of this section, on or after the date on which the license was issued, the licensee is convicted of or pleads guilty to a violation of section 2923.15 of the Revised Code or an offense described in division (D)(1)(e), (f), (g), or (h) of section 2923.125 of the Revised Code.

(d) On or after the date on which the license was issued, the licensee becomes subject to a civil protection order or to a protection order issued by a court of another state that is substantially equivalent to a civil protection order.

(e) The licensee knowingly carries a concealed handgun into a place that the licensee knows is an unauthorized place specified in division (B) of section 2923.126 of the Revised Code.

(f) On or after the date on which the license was issued, the licensee is adjudicated as a mental defective or is committed to a mental institution.

(g) At the time of the issuance of the license, the licensee did not meet the residency requirements described in division (D)(1) of section 2923.125 of the Revised Code and currently does not meet the residency requirements described in that division.

(h) Regarding a license issued under section 2923.125 of the Revised Code, the competency certificate the licensee submitted was forged or otherwise was fraudulent.

(2) Upon becoming aware of any circumstance listed in division (B)(1) of this section that applies to a particular licensee who was issued a concealed handgun license, subject to division (C) of this section, the sheriff who issued the license to the licensee shall notify the licensee, by certified mail, return receipt requested, at the licensee's last known residence address that the license is subject to revocation and that the licensee may come to the sheriff's office and contest the sheriff's proposed revocation within fourteen days of the date on which the notice was mailed. After the fourteen-day period and after consideration of any information that the licensee provides during that period, if the sheriff determines on the basis of the information of which the sheriff is aware that the licensee is described in division (B)(1) of this section and no longer satisfies the requirements described in division (D)(1) of section 2923.125 of the Revised Code that are applicable to the licensee's type of license, the sheriff shall revoke the license, notify the licensee of that fact, and require the licensee to surrender the license. Upon revoking the license, the sheriff also shall comply with division (H) of section 2923.125 of the Revised Code.

(C) If a sheriff who issues a concealed handgun license to a licensee becomes aware that at the time of the issuance of the license the licensee had been convicted of or pleaded guilty to an offense identified in division (D)(1)(e), (f), or (h) of section 2923.125 of the Revised Code or had been adjudicated a delinquent child for committing an act or violation identified in any of those divisions or becomes aware that on or after the date on which the license was issued the licensee has been convicted of or pleaded guilty to an offense identified in division (A)(2)(a) or (B)(1)(c) of this section, the sheriff shall not consider that conviction, guilty plea, or adjudication as having occurred for purposes of divisions (A)(2), (A)(3), (B)(1), and (B)(2) of this section if a court has ordered the sealing or expungement of the records of that conviction, guilty plea, or adjudication pursuant to sections 2151.355 to 2151.358 or sections 2953.31 to 2953.36 of the Revised Code or the licensee has been relieved under operation of law or legal process from the disability imposed pursuant to section 2923.13 of the Revised Code relative to that conviction, guilty plea, or adjudication.

(D) As used in this section, "motor carrier enforcement unit" has the same meaning as in section 2923.16 of the Revised Code.

2923.129 Immunity.

(A)(1) If a sheriff, the superintendent of the bureau of criminal identification and investigation, the employees of the bureau, the Ohio peace officer training commission, or the employees of the commission make a good faith effort in performing the duties imposed upon the sheriff, the superintendent, the bureau's employees, the commission, or the commission's employees by sections 109.731, 311.41, and 2923.124 to 2923.1213 of the Revised Code, in addition to the personal immunity provided by section 9.86 of the Revised Code or division (A)(6) of section 2744.03 of the Revised Code and the governmental immunity of sections 2744.02 and 2744.03 of the Revised Code and in addition to any other immunity possessed by the bureau, the commission, and their employees, the sheriff, the sheriff's office, the county in which the sheriff has jurisdiction, the bureau, the superintendent of the bureau, the bureau's employees, the commission, and the commission's employees are immune from liability in a civil action for injury, death, or loss to person or property that allegedly was caused by or related to any of the following:

(a) The issuance, renewal, suspension, or revocation of a concealed handgun license;

(b) The failure to issue, renew, suspend, or revoke a concealed handgun license;

(c) Any action or misconduct with a handgun committed by a licensee.

(2) Any action of a sheriff relating to the issuance, renewal, suspension, or revocation of a concealed handgun license shall be considered to be a governmental function for purposes of Chapter 2744. of the Revised Code.

(3) An entity that or instructor who provides a competency certification of a type described in division (B)(3) of section 2923.125 of the Revised Code is immune from civil liability that might otherwise be incurred or imposed for any death or any injury or loss to person or property that is caused by or related to a person to whom the entity or instructor has issued the competency certificate if all of the following apply:

(a) The alleged liability of the entity or instructor relates to the training provided in the course, class, or program covered by the competency certificate.

(b) The entity or instructor makes a good faith effort in determining whether the person has satisfactorily completed the course, class, or program and makes a good faith effort in assessing the person in the competency examination conducted pursuant to division (G)(2) of section 2923.125 of the Revised Code.

(c) The entity or instructor did not issue the competency certificate with malicious purpose, in bad faith, or in a wanton or reckless manner.

(4) An entity that or instructor who, prior to March 27, 2013, provides a renewed competency certification of a type described in division (G)(4) of section 2923.125 of the Revised Code as it existed prior to March 27, 2013, is immune from civil liability that might otherwise be incurred or imposed for any death or any injury or loss to person or property that is caused by or related to a person to whom the entity or instructor has issued the renewed competency certificate if all of the following apply:

(a) The entity or instructor makes a good faith effort in assessing the person in the physical demonstrations or the competency examination conducted pursuant to division (G)(4) of section 2923.125 of the Revised Code as it existed prior to March 27, 2013.

(b) The entity or instructor did not issue the renewed competency certificate with malicious purpose, in bad faith, or in a wanton or reckless manner.

(5) A law enforcement agency that employs a peace officer is immune from liability in a civil action to recover damages for injury, death, or loss to person or property allegedly caused by any act of that peace officer if the act occurred while the peace officer carried a concealed handgun and was off duty and if the act allegedly involved the peace officer's use of the concealed handgun. Sections 9.86 and 9.87, and Chapter 2744., of the Revised Code apply to any civil action involving a peace officer's use of a concealed handgun in the performance of the peace officer's official duties while the peace officer is off duty.

(B) Notwithstanding section 149.43 of the Revised Code, the records that a sheriff keeps relative to the issuance, renewal, suspension, or revocation of a concealed handgun license, including, but not limited to, completed applications for the issuance or renewal of a license, completed affidavits submitted regarding an application for a license on a temporary emergency basis, reports of criminal records checks and incompetency records checks under section 311.41 of the Revised Code, and applicants' social security numbers and fingerprints that are obtained under division (A) of section

311.41 of the Revised Code, are confidential and are not public records. No person shall release or otherwise disseminate records that are confidential under this division unless required to do so pursuant to a court order.

(C) Each sheriff shall report to the Ohio peace officer training commission the number of concealed handgun licenses that the sheriff issued, renewed, suspended, revoked, or denied under section 2923.125 of the Revised Code during the previous quarter of the calendar year, the number of applications for those licenses for which processing was suspended in accordance with division (D)(3) of section 2923.125 of the Revised Code during the previous quarter of the calendar year, and the number of concealed handgun licenses on a temporary emergency basis that the sheriff issued, suspended, revoked, or denied under section 2923.1213 of the Revised Code during the previous quarter of the calendar year. The sheriff shall not include in the report the name or any other identifying information of an applicant or licensee. The sheriff shall report that information in a manner that permits the commission to maintain the statistics described in division (C) of section 109.731 of the Revised Code and to timely prepare the statistical report described in that division. The information that is received by the commission under this division is a public record kept by the commission for the purposes of section 149.43 of the Revised Code.

(D) Law enforcement agencies may use the information a sheriff makes available through the use of the law enforcement automated data system pursuant to division (H) of section 2923.125 or division (B)(2) or (D) of section 2923.1213 of the Revised Code for law enforcement purposes only. The information is confidential and is not a public record. A person who releases or otherwise disseminates this information obtained through the law enforcement automated data system in a manner not described in this division is guilty of a violation of section 2913.04 of the Revised Code.

(E) Whoever violates division (B) of this section is guilty of illegal release of confidential concealed handgun license records, a felony of the fifth degree. In addition to any penalties imposed under

Chapter 2929. of the Revised Code for a violation of division (B) of this section or a violation of section 2913.04 of the Revised Code described in division (D) of this section, if the offender is a sheriff, an employee of a sheriff, or any other public officer or employee, and if the violation was willful and deliberate, the offender shall be subject to a civil fine of one thousand dollars. Any person who is harmed by a violation of division (B) or (C) of this section or a violation of section 2913.04 of the Revised Code described in division (D) of this section has a private cause of action against the offender for any injury, death, or loss to person or property that is a proximate result of the violation and may recover court costs and attorney's fees related to the action.

2923.1211 Falsification of concealed handgun license - possessing a revoked or suspended concealed handgun license.

(A) No person shall alter a concealed handgun license or create a fictitious document that purports to be a license of that nature.

(B) No person, except in the performance of official duties, shall possess a concealed handgun license that was issued and that has been revoked or suspended.

(C) Whoever violates division (A) of this section is guilty of falsification of a concealed handgun license, a felony of the fifth degree. Whoever violates division (B) of this section is guilty of possessing a revoked or suspended concealed handgun license, a misdemeanor of the third degree.

2923.1213 Temporary emergency license.

(A) As used in this section:

(1) "Evidence of imminent danger" means any of the following:

(a) A statement sworn by the person seeking to carry a concealed handgun that is made under threat of perjury and that states that the person has reasonable cause to fear a criminal attack upon the person or a member of the person's family, such as would justify a prudent person in going armed;

(b) A written document prepared by a governmental entity or public official describing the facts that give the person seeking to carry a concealed handgun reasonable cause to fear a criminal attack upon the person or a member of the person's family, such as would justify a prudent person in going armed. Written documents of this nature include, but are not limited to, any temporary protection order, civil protection order, protection order issued by another state, or other court order, any court report, and any report filed with or made by a law enforcement agency or prosecutor.

(2) "Prosecutor" has the same meaning as in section 2935.01 of the Revised Code.

(B)(1) A person seeking a concealed handgun license on a temporary emergency basis shall submit to the sheriff of the county in which the person resides or, if the person usually resides in another state, to the sheriff of the county in which the person is temporarily staying, all of the following:

(a) Evidence of imminent danger to the person or a member of the person's family;

(b) A sworn affidavit that contains all of the information required to be on the license and attesting that the person is legally living in the United States; is at least twenty-one years of age; is not a fugitive from justice; is not under indictment for or otherwise charged with an offense identified in division (D)(1)(d) of section 2923.125 of the Revised Code; has not been convicted of or pleaded guilty to an offense, and has not been adjudicated a delinquent child for committing an act, identified in division (D)(1)(e) of that section and to which division (B)(3) of this section does not apply; within three years of the date of the submission, has not been convicted of or pleaded guilty to an offense, and has not been adjudicated a delinquent child for committing an act, identified in division (D)(1)(f) of that section and to which division (B)(3) of this section does not apply; within five years of the date of the submission, has not been convicted of, pleaded guilty, or adjudicated a delinquent child for committing two or more violations identified in division (D)(1)(g) of that section; within ten years of the date of the submission, has not been convicted of, pleaded guilty, or adjudicated a delinquent child for committing a violation identified in division (D)(1)(h) of that section and to which division (B)(3) of this section does not apply; has not been adjudicated as a mental defective, has not been committed to any mental institution, is not under adjudication of mental incompetence, has not been found by a court to be a mentally ill person subject to court order, and is not an involuntary patient other than one who is a patient only for purposes of observation, as described in division (D)(1)(i) of that section; is not currently subject to a civil protection order, a temporary protection order, or a protection order issued by a court of another state, as described in division (D)(1) (j) of that section; is not currently subject to a suspension imposed under division (A)(2) of section 2923.128 of the Revised Code of a concealed handgun license that previously was issued to the person or a similar suspension imposed by another state regarding a concealed handgun license issued by that state; is not an unlawful user of or addicted to any controlled substance as defined in 21 U.S.C. 802; if applicable, is an alien and has not been admitted to the United States under a nonimmigrant visa, as defined in the "Immigration and Nationality Act," 8 U.S.C. 1101(a)(26); has not been discharged from the armed forces of the United States under dishonorable conditions; if applicable, has not renounced the applicant's United States citizenship; and has not been convicted of, pleaded guilty to, or been adjudicated a delinquent child for committing a violation identified in division (D)(1)(s) of section 2923.125 of the Revised Code;

(c) A nonrefundable temporary emergency license fee as described in either of the following:

(i) For an applicant who has been a resident of this state for five or more years, a fee of fifteen dollars plus the actual cost of having a background check performed by the bureau of criminal identification and investigation pursuant to section 311.41 of the Revised Code;

(ii) For an applicant who has been a resident of this state for less than five years or who is not a resident of this state, but is temporarily staying in this state, a fee of fifteen dollars plus the actual cost of having background checks performed by the federal bureau of investigation and the bureau of criminal identification and investigation pursuant to section 311.41 of the Revised Code.

(d) A set of fingerprints of the applicant provided as described in section 311.41 of the Revised Code through use of an electronic fingerprint reading device or, if the sheriff to whom the application is submitted does not possess and does not have ready access to the use of an electronic fingerprint reading device, on a standard impression sheet prescribed pursuant to division (C)(2) of section 109.572 of the Revised Code. If the fingerprints are provided on a standard impression sheet, the person also shall provide the person's social security number to the sheriff.

(2) A sheriff shall accept the evidence of imminent danger, the sworn affidavit, the fee, and the set of fingerprints required under division (B)(1) of this section at the times and in the manners described in division (I) of this section. Upon receipt of the evidence of imminent danger, the sworn affidavit, the fee, and the set of fingerprints required under division (B)(1) of this section, the sheriff, in the manner specified in section 311.41 of the Revised Code, immediately shall conduct or cause to be conducted the criminal records check and the incompetency records check described in section 311.41 of the Revised Code. Immediately upon receipt of the results of the records checks, the sheriff shall review the information and shall determine whether the criteria set forth in divisions (D)(1)(a) to (j) and (m) to (s) of section 2923.125 of the Revised Code apply regarding the person. If the sheriff determines that all of criteria set forth in divisions (D)(1)(a) to (j) and (m) to (s) of section 2923.125 of the Revised Code apply regarding the person, the sheriff shall immediately make available through the law enforcement automated data system all information that will be contained on the temporary emergency license for the person if one is issued, and the superintendent of the state highway patrol shall ensure that the system is so configured as to permit the transmission through the system of that

information. Upon making that information available through the law enforcement automated data system, the sheriff shall immediately issue to the person a concealed handgun license on a temporary emergency basis.

If the sheriff denies the issuance of a license on a temporary emergency basis to the person, the sheriff shall specify the grounds for the denial in a written notice to the person. The person may appeal the denial, or challenge criminal records check results that were the basis of the denial if applicable, in the same manners specified in division (D)(2) of section 2923.125 and in section 2923.127 of the Revised Code, regarding the denial of an application for a concealed handgun license under that section.

The license on a temporary emergency basis issued under this division shall be in the form, and shall include all of the information, described in divisions (A)(2)(a) and (d) of section 109.731 of the Revised Code, and also shall include a unique combination of identifying letters and numbers in accordance with division (A) (2)(c) of that section.

The license on a temporary emergency basis issued under this division is valid for ninety days and may not be renewed. A person who has been issued a license on a temporary emergency basis under this division shall not be issued another license on a temporary emergency basis unless at least four years has expired since the issuance of the prior license on a temporary emergency basis.

(3) If a person seeking a concealed handgun license on a temporary emergency basis has been convicted of or pleaded guilty to an offense identified in division (D)(1)(e), (f), or (h) of section 2923.125 of the Revised Code or has been adjudicated a delinquent child for committing an act or violation identified in any of those divisions, and if a court has ordered the sealing or expungement of the records of that conviction, guilty plea, or adjudication pursuant to sections 2151.355 to 2151.358 or sections 2953.31 to 2953.36 of the Revised Code or the applicant has been relieved under operation of law or legal process from the disability imposed pursuant to section 2923.13 of the Revised Code relative to that conviction, guilty plea,

or adjudication, the conviction, guilty plea, or adjudication shall not be relevant for purposes of the sworn affidavit described in division (B)(1)(b) of this section, and the person may complete, and swear to the truth of, the affidavit as if the conviction, guilty plea, or adjudication never had occurred.

(4) The sheriff shall waive the payment pursuant to division (B)(1)(c) of this section of the license fee in connection with an application that is submitted by an applicant who is a retired peace officer, a retired person described in division (B)(1)(b) of section 109.77 of the Revised Code, or a retired federal law enforcement officer who, prior to retirement, was authorized under federal law to carry a firearm in the course of duty, unless the retired peace officer, person, or federal law enforcement officer retired as the result of a mental disability.

The sheriff shall deposit all fees paid by an applicant under division (B)(1)(c) of this section into the sheriff's concealed handgun license issuance fund established pursuant to section 311.42 of the Revised Code.

(C) A person who holds a concealed handgun license on a temporary emergency basis has the same right to carry a concealed handgun as a person who was issued a concealed handgun license under section 2923.125 of the Revised Code, and any exceptions to the prohibitions contained in section 1547.69 and sections 2923.12 to 2923.16 of the Revised Code for a licensee under section 2923.125 of the Revised Code apply to a licensee under this section. The person is subject to the same restrictions, and to all other procedures, duties, and sanctions, that apply to a person who carries a license issued under section 2923.125 of the Revised Code, other than the license renewal procedures set forth in that section.

(D) A sheriff who issues a concealed handgun license on a temporary emergency basis under this section shall not require a person seeking to carry a concealed handgun in accordance with this section to submit a competency certificate as a prerequisite for issuing the license and shall comply with division (H) of section 2923.125

of the Revised Code in regards to the license. The sheriff shall suspend or revoke the license in accordance with section 2923.128 of the Revised Code. In addition to the suspension or revocation procedures set forth in section 2923.128 of the Revised Code, the sheriff may revoke the license upon receiving information, verifiable by public documents, that the person is not eligible to possess a firearm under either the laws of this state or of the United States or that the person committed perjury in obtaining the license; if the sheriff revokes a license under this additional authority, the sheriff shall notify the person, by certified mail, return receipt requested, at the person's last known residence address that the license has been revoked and that the person is required to surrender the license at the sheriff's office within ten days of the date on which the notice was mailed. Division (H) of section 2923.125 of the Revised Code applies regarding any suspension or revocation of a concealed handgun license on a temporary emergency basis.

(E) A sheriff who issues a concealed handgun license on a temporary emergency basis under this section shall retain, for the entire period during which the license is in effect, the evidence of imminent danger that the person submitted to the sheriff and that was the basis for the license, or a copy of that evidence, as appropriate.

(F) If a concealed handgun license on a temporary emergency basis issued under this section is lost or is destroyed, the licensee may obtain from the sheriff who issued that license a duplicate license upon the payment of a fee of fifteen dollars and the submission of an affidavit attesting to the loss or destruction of the license. The sheriff, in accordance with the procedures prescribed in section 109.731 of the Revised Code, shall place on the replacement license a combination of identifying numbers different from the combination on the license that is being replaced.

(G) The attorney general shall prescribe, and shall make available to sheriffs, a standard form to be used under division (B) of this section by a person who applies for a concealed handgun license on a temporary emergency basis on the basis of imminent danger of a type described in division (A)(1)(a) of this section. The attorney general shall design the form to enable applicants to provide the information that is required by law to be collected, and shall update the form as necessary. Burdens or restrictions to obtaining a concealed handgun license that are not expressly prescribed in law shall not be incorporated into the form. The attorney general shall post a printable version of the form on the web site of the attorney general and shall provide the address of the web site to any person who requests the form.

(H) A sheriff who receives any fees paid by a person under this section shall deposit all fees so paid into the sheriff's concealed handgun license issuance expense fund established under section 311.42 of the Revised Code.

(I) A sheriff shall accept evidence of imminent danger, a sworn affidavit, the fee, and the set of fingerprints specified in division (B)(1) of this section at any time during normal business hours. In no case shall a sheriff require an appointment, or designate a specific period of time, for the submission or acceptance of evidence of imminent danger, a sworn affidavit, the fee, and the set of fingerprints specified in division (B)(1) of this section, or for the provision to any person of a standard form to be used for a person to apply for a concealed handgun license on a temporary emergency basis.

2923.13 Having weapons while under disability.

(A) Unless relieved from disability under operation of law or legal process, no person shall knowingly acquire, have, carry, or use any firearm or dangerous ordnance, if any of the following apply:

(1) The person is a fugitive from justice.

(2) The person is under indictment for or has been convicted of any felony offense of violence or has been adjudicated a delinquent child for the commission of an offense that, if committed by an adult, would have been a felony offense of violence.

(3) The person is under indictment for or has been convicted of any felony offense involving the illegal possession, use, sale,

administration, distribution, or trafficking in any drug of abuse or has been adjudicated a delinquent child for the commission of an offense that, if committed by an adult, would have been a felony offense involving the illegal possession, use, sale, administration, distribution, or trafficking in any drug of abuse.

(4) The person is drug dependent, in danger of drug dependence, or a chronic alcoholic.

(5) The person is under adjudication of mental incompetence, has been adjudicated as a mental defective, has been committed to a mental institution, has been found by a court to be a mentally ill person subject to court order, or is an involuntary patient other than one who is a patient only for purposes of observation. As used in this division, "mentally ill person subject to court order" and "patient" have the same meanings as in section 5122.01 of the Revised Code.

(B) Whoever violates this section is guilty of having weapons while under disability, a felony of the third degree.

(C) For the purposes of this section, "under operation of law or legal process" shall not itself include mere completion, termination, or expiration of a sentence imposed as a result of a criminal conviction.

2923.14 Relief from weapons disability.

(A) Any person who is prohibited from acquiring, having, carrying, or using firearms may apply to the court of common pleas in the county in which the person resides for relief from such prohibition.

(B) The application shall recite the following:

(1) All indictments, convictions, or adjudications upon which the applicant's disability is based, the sentence imposed and served, and any release granted under a community control sanction, post-release control sanction, or parole, any partial or conditional pardon granted, or other disposition of each case, or, if the disability is based upon a factor other than an indictment, a conviction, or an

adjudication, the factor upon which the disability is based and all details related to that factor;

(2) Facts showing the applicant to be a fit subject for relief under this section.

(C) A copy of the application shall be served on the county prosecutor. The county prosecutor shall cause the matter to be investigated and shall raise before the court any objections to granting relief that the investigation reveals.

(D) Upon hearing, the court may grant the applicant relief pursuant to this section, if all of the following apply:

(1) One of the following applies:

(a) If the disability is based upon an indictment, a conviction, or an adjudication, the applicant has been fully discharged from imprisonment, community control, post-release control, and parole, or, if the applicant is under indictment, has been released on bail or recognizance.

(b) If the disability is based upon a factor other than an indictment, a conviction, or an adjudication, that factor no longer is applicable to the applicant.

(2) The applicant has led a law-abiding life since discharge or release, and appears likely to continue to do so.

(3) The applicant is not otherwise prohibited by law from acquiring, having, or using firearms.

(E) Costs of the proceeding shall be charged as in other civil cases, and taxed to the applicant.

(F) Relief from disability granted pursuant to this section restores the applicant to all civil firearm rights to the full extent enjoyed by any citizen, and is subject to the following conditions:

(1) Applies only with respect to indictments, convictions, or adjudications, or to the other factor, recited in the application as the basis for the applicant's disability;

(2) Applies only with respect to firearms lawfully acquired, possessed, carried, or used by the applicant;

(3)May be revoked by the court at any time for good cause shown and upon notice to the applicant;

(4) Is automatically void upon commission by the applicant of any offense set forth in division (A)(2) or (3) of section 2923.13 of the Revised Code, or upon the applicant's becoming one of the class of persons named in division (A)(1), (4), or (5) of that section.

(G) As used in this section:

(1) "Community control sanction" has the same meaning as in section 2929.01 of the Revised Code.

(2) "Post-release control" and "post-release control sanction" have the same meanings as in section 2967.01 of the Revised Code.

2923.15 Using weapons while intoxicated.

(A) No person, while under the influence of alcohol or any drug of abuse, shall carry or use any firearm or dangerous ordnance.

(B) Whoever violates this section is guilty of using weapons while intoxicated, a misdemeanor of the first degree.

2923.16 Improperly handling firearms in a motor vehicle.

(A) No person shall knowingly discharge a firearm while in or on a motor vehicle.

(B) No person shall knowingly transport or have a loaded firearm in a motor vehicle in such a manner that the firearm is accessible to the operator or any passenger without leaving the vehicle.

(C) No person shall knowingly transport or have a firearm in a motor vehicle, unless the person may lawfully possess that firearm under applicable law of this state or the United States, the firearm is unloaded, and the firearm is carried in one of the following ways:

(1) In a closed package, box, or case;

(2) In a compartment that can be reached only by leaving the vehicle;

(3) In plain sight and secured in a rack or holder made for the purpose;

(4) If the firearm is at least twenty-four inches in overall length as measured from the muzzle to the part of the stock furthest from the muzzle and if the barrel is at least eighteen inches in length, either in plain sight with the action open or the weapon stripped, or, if the firearm is of a type on which the action will not stay open or which cannot easily be stripped, in plain sight.

(D) No person shall knowingly transport or have a loaded handgun in a motor vehicle if, at the time of that transportation or possession, any of the following applies:

(1) The person is under the influence of alcohol, a drug of abuse, or a combination of them.

(2) The person's whole blood, blood serum or plasma, breath, or urine contains a concentration of alcohol, a listed controlled substance, or a listed metabolite of a controlled substance prohibited for persons operating a vehicle, as specified in division (A) of section 4511.19 of the Revised Code, regardless of whether the person at the time of the transportation or possession as described in this division is the operator of or a passenger in the motor vehicle.

(E) No person who has been issued a concealed handgun license, who is the driver or an occupant of a motor vehicle that is stopped as a result of a traffic stop or a stop for another law enforcement purpose or is the driver or an occupant of a commercial motor vehicle that is stopped by an employee of the motor carrier enforcement unit for the purposes defined in section 5503.34 of the Revised Code, and who is transporting or has a loaded handgun in the motor vehicle or commercial motor vehicle in any manner, shall do any of the following:

(1) Fail to promptly inform any law enforcement officer who approaches the vehicle while stopped that the person has been issued a concealed handgun license and that the person then possesses or has a loaded handgun in the motor vehicle;

(2) Fail to promptly inform the employee of the unit who approaches the vehicle while stopped that the person has been issued a concealed handgun license and that the person then possesses or has a loaded handgun in the commercial motor vehicle;

(3) Knowingly fail to remain in the motor vehicle while stopped or knowingly fail to keep the person's hands in plain sight at any time after any law enforcement officer begins approaching the person while stopped and before the law enforcement officer leaves, unless the failure is pursuant to and in accordance with directions given by a law enforcement officer;

(4) Knowingly have contact with the loaded handgun by touching it with the person's hands or fingers in the motor vehicle at any time after the law enforcement officer begins approaching and before the law enforcement officer leaves, unless the person has contact with the loaded handgun pursuant to and in accordance with directions given by the law enforcement officer;

(5) Knowingly disregard or fail to comply with any lawful order of any law enforcement officer given while the motor vehicle is stopped, including, but not limited to, a specific order to the person to keep the person's hands in plain sight.

(F)(1) Divisions (A), (B), (C), and (E) of this section do not apply to any of the following:

(a) An officer, agent, or employee of this or any other state or the United States, or a law enforcement officer, when authorized to carry or have loaded or accessible firearms in motor vehicles and acting within the scope of the officer's, agent's, or employee's duties;

(b) Any person who is employed in this state, who is authorized to carry or have loaded or accessible firearms in motor vehicles, and who is subject to and in compliance with the requirements of section 109.801 of the Revised Code, unless the appointing authority of the person has expressly specified that the exemption provided in division (F)(1)(b) of this section does not apply to the person.

(2) Division (A) of this section does not apply to a person if all of the following circumstances apply:

(a) The person discharges a firearm from a motor vehicle at a coyote or groundhog, the discharge is not during the deer gun hunting season as set by the chief of the division of wildlife of the department of natural resources, and the discharge at the coyote or groundhog, but for the operation of this section, is lawful.

(b) The motor vehicle from which the person discharges the firearm is on real property that is located in an unincorporated area of a township and that either is zoned for agriculture or is used for agriculture.

(c) The person owns the real property described in division (F)(2)(b) of this section, is the spouse or a child of another person who owns that real property, is a tenant of another person who owns that real property, or is the spouse or a child of a tenant of another person who owns that real property.

(d) The person does not discharge the firearm in any of the following manners:

(i) While under the influence of alcohol, a drug of abuse, or alcohol and a drug of abuse;

(ii) In the direction of a street, highway, or other public or private property used by the public for vehicular traffic or parking;

(iii) At or into an occupied structure that is a permanent or temporary habitation;

(iv) In the commission of any violation of law, including, but not limited to, a felony that includes, as an essential element, purposely or knowingly causing or attempting to cause the death of or physical harm to another and that was committed by discharging a firearm from a motor vehicle.

(3) Division (A) of this section does not apply to a person if all of the following apply:

(a) The person possesses a valid electric-powered all-purpose vehicle permit issued under section 1533.103 of the Revised Code by the chief of the division of wildlife.

(b) The person discharges a firearm at a wild quadruped or game bird as defined in section 1531.01 of the Revised Code during the open hunting season for the applicable wild quadruped or game bird.

(c) The person discharges a firearm from a stationary electric-powered all-purpose vehicle as defined in section 1531.01 of the Revised Code or a motor vehicle that is parked on a road that is owned or administered by the division of wildlife, provided that the road is identified by an electric-powered all-purpose vehicle sign.

(d) The person does not discharge the firearm in any of the following manners:

(i) While under the influence of alcohol, a drug of abuse, or alcohol and a drug of abuse;

(ii) In the direction of a street, a highway, or other public or private property that is used by the public for vehicular traffic or parking;

(iii) At or into an occupied structure that is a permanent or temporary habitation;

(iv) In the commission of any violation of law, including, but not limited to, a felony that includes, as an essential element, purposely or knowingly causing or attempting to cause the death of or physical harm to another and that was committed by discharging a firearm from a motor vehicle.

(4) Divisions (B) and (C) of this section do not apply to a person if all of the following circumstances apply:

(a) At the time of the alleged violation of either of those divisions, the person is the operator of or a passenger in a motor vehicle.

(b) The motor vehicle is on real property that is located in an unincorporated area of a township and that either is zoned for agriculture or is used for agriculture.

(c) The person owns the real property described in division (D)(4) (b) of this section, is the spouse or a child of another person who owns that real property, is a tenant of another person who owns that real property, or is the spouse or a child of a tenant of another person who owns that real property.

(d) The person, prior to arriving at the real property described in division (D)(4)(b) of this section, did not transport or possess a firearm in the motor vehicle in a manner prohibited by division (B) or (C) of this section while the motor vehicle was being operated on a street, highway, or other public or private property used by the public for vehicular traffic or parking.

(5) Divisions (B) and (C) of this section do not apply to a person who transports or possesses a handgun in a motor vehicle if, at the time of that transportation or possession, both of the following apply:

(a) The person transporting or possessing the handgun is carrying a valid concealed handgun license.

(b) The person transporting or possessing the handgun is not knowingly in a place described in division (B) of section 2923.126 of the Revised Code.

(6) Divisions (B) and (C) of this section do not apply to a person if all of the following apply:

(a) The person possesses a valid electric-powered all-purpose vehicle permit issued under section 1533.103 of the Revised Code by the chief of the division of wildlife.

(b) The person is on or in an electric-powered all-purpose vehicle as defined in section 1531.01 of the Revised Code or a motor vehicle during the open hunting season for a wild quadruped or game bird.

(c) The person is on or in an electric-powered all-purpose vehicle as defined in section 1531.01 of the Revised Code or a motor vehicle that is parked on a road that is owned or administered by the division of wildlife, provided that the road is identified by an electric-powered all-purpose vehicle sign.

(7) Nothing in this section prohibits or restricts a person from possessing, storing, or leaving a firearm in a locked motor vehicle that is parked in the state underground parking garage at the state capitol building or in the parking garage at the Riffe center for government and the arts in Columbus, if the person's transportation and possession of the firearm in the motor vehicle while traveling to the premises or facility was not in violation of division (A), (B), (C), (D), or (E) of this section or any other provision of the Revised Code.

(G)(1) The affirmative defenses authorized in divisions (D)(1) and (2) of section 2923.12 of the Revised Code are affirmative defenses to a charge under division (B) or (C) of this section that involves a firearm other than a handgun.

(2) It is an affirmative defense to a charge under division (B) or (C) of this section of improperly handling firearms in a motor vehicle that the actor transported or had the firearm in the motor vehicle for any lawful purpose and while the motor vehicle was on the actor's own property, provided that this affirmative defense is not available unless the person, immediately prior to arriving at the actor's own property, did not transport or possess the firearm in a motor vehicle in a manner prohibited by division (B) or (C) of this section while the motor vehicle was being operated on a street, highway, or other public or private property used by the public for vehicular traffic.

(H)(1) No person who is charged with a violation of division (B), (C), or (D) of this section shall be required to obtain a concealed handgun license as a condition for the dismissal of the charge.

(2)(a) If a person is convicted of, was convicted of, pleads guilty to, or has pleaded guilty to a violation of division (E) of this section as it existed prior to September 30, 2011, and if the conduct that was the basis of the violation no longer would be a violation of division (E) of this section on or after September 30, 2011, the person may file an application under section 2953.37 of the Revised Code requesting the expungement of the record of conviction.

If a person is convicted of, was convicted of, pleads guilty to, or has pleaded guilty to a violation of division (B) or (C) of this section as the division existed prior to September 30, 2011, and if the conduct that was the basis of the violation no longer would be a violation of division (B) or (C) of this section on or after September 30, 2011, due to the application of division (F)(5) of this section as it exists on and after September 30, 2011, the person may file an application under section 2953.37 of the Revised Code requesting the expungement of the record of conviction.

(b) The attorney general shall develop a public media advisory that summarizes the expungement procedure established under section 2953.37 of the Revised Code and the offenders identified in division (H)(2)(a) of this section who are authorized to apply for the expungement. Within thirty days after September 30, 2011, the attorney general shall provide a copy of the advisory to each daily newspaper published in this state and each television station that broadcasts in this state. The attorney general may provide the advisory in a tangible form, an electronic form, or in both tangible and electronic forms.

(I) Whoever violates this section is guilty of improperly handling firearms in a motor vehicle. Violation of division (A) of this section is a felony of the fourth degree. Violation of division (C) of this section is a misdemeanor of the fourth degree. A violation of division (D) of this section is a felony of the fifth degree or, if the loaded handgun is concealed on the person's person, a felony of the fourth degree. Except as otherwise provided in this division, a violation of division (E)(1) or (2) of this section is a misdemeanor of the first degree, and, in addition to any other penalty or sanction imposed for the violation, the offender's concealed handgun license shall be suspended pursuant to division (A)(2) of section 2923.128 of the Revised Code. If at the time of the stop of the offender for a traffic stop, for another law enforcement purpose, or for a purpose defined in section 5503.34 of the Revised Code that was the basis of the violation any law enforcement officer involved with the stop or the employee of the motor carrier enforcement unit who made the stop had actual knowledge of the offender's status as a licensee, a violation of division (E)(1) or (2) of this section is a minor misdemeanor, and the offender's concealed handgun license shall not be suspended pursuant to division (A)(2) of section 2923.128 of the Revised Code. A violation of division (E)(4) of this section is a felony of the fifth degree. A violation of division (E)(3) or (5) of this section is a misdemeanor of the first degree or, if the offender previously has been convicted of or pleaded guilty to a violation of division (E)(3) or (5) of this section, a felony of the fifth degree. In addition to any other penalty or sanction imposed for a misdemeanor violation of division (E)(3) or (5) of this section, the offender's concealed handgun license shall be suspended pursuant to division (A)(2) of section 2923.128 of the Revised Code. A violation of division (B) of this section is a felony of the fourth degree.

(J) If a law enforcement officer stops a motor vehicle for a traffic stop or any other purpose, if any person in the motor vehicle surrenders a firearm to the officer, either voluntarily or pursuant to a request or demand of the officer, and if the officer does not charge the person with a violation of this section or arrest the person for any offense, the person is not otherwise prohibited by law from possessing the firearm, and the firearm is not contraband, the officer shall return the firearm to the person at the termination of the stop. If a court orders a law enforcement officer to return a firearm to a person pursuant to the requirement set forth in this division, division (B) of section 2923.163 of the Revised Code applies.

(K) As used in this section:

(1) "Motor vehicle," "street," and "highway" have the same meanings as in section 4511.01 of the Revised Code.

(2) "Occupied structure" has the same meaning as in section 2909.01 of the Revised Code.

(3) "Agriculture" has the same meaning as in section 519.01 of the Revised Code.

(4) "Tenant" has the same meaning as in section 1531.01 of the Revised Code.

(5)(a) "Unloaded" means, with respect to a firearm other than a firearm described in division (K)(6) of this section, that no ammunition is in the firearm in question, no magazine or speed loader containing ammunition is inserted into the firearm in question, and one of the following applies:

(i) There is no ammunition in a magazine or speed loader that is in the vehicle in question and that may be used with the firearm in question.

(ii) Any magazine or speed loader that contains ammunition and that may be used with the firearm in question is stored in a compartment within the vehicle in question that cannot be accessed without leaving the vehicle or is stored in a container that provides complete and separate enclosure.

(b) For the purposes of division (K)(5)(a)(ii) of this section, a "container that provides complete and separate enclosure" includes, but is not limited to, any of the following:

(i) A package, box, or case with multiple compartments, as long as the loaded magazine or speed loader and the firearm in question either are in separate compartments within the package, box, or case, or, if they are in the same compartment, the magazine or speed loader is contained within a separate enclosure in that compartment that does not contain the firearm and that closes using a snap, button, buckle, zipper, hook and loop closing mechanism, or other fastener that must be opened to access the contents or the firearm is contained within a separate enclosure of that nature in that compartment that does not contain the magazine or speed loader;

(ii) A pocket or other enclosure on the person of the person in question that closes using a snap, button, buckle, zipper, hook and loop closing mechanism, or other fastener that must be opened to access the contents.

(c) For the purposes of divisions (K)(5)(a) and (b) of this section, ammunition held in stripper-clips or in en-bloc clips is not considered ammunition that is loaded into a magazine or speed loader.

(6) "Unloaded" means, with respect to a firearm employing a percussion cap, flintlock, or other obsolete ignition system, when the weapon is uncapped or when the priming charge is removed from the pan.

(7) "Commercial motor vehicle" has the same meaning as in division (A) of section 4506.25 of the Revised Code.

(8) "Motor carrier enforcement unit" means the motor carrier enforcement unit in the department of public safety, division of state highway patrol, that is created by section 5503.34 of the Revised Code.

(L) Divisions (K)(5)(a) and (b) of this section do not affect the authority of a person who is carrying a valid concealed handgun license to have one or more magazines or speed loaders containing ammunition anywhere in a vehicle, without being transported as described in those divisions, as long as no ammunition is in a firearm, other than a handgun, in the vehicle other than as permitted under any other provision of this chapter. A person who is carrying a valid concealed handgun license may have one or more magazines or speed loaders containing ammunition anywhere in a vehicle without further restriction, as long as no ammunition is in a firearm, other than a handgun, in the vehicle other than as permitted under any provision of this chapter.

2923.161 Improperly discharging firearm at or into a habitation, in a school safety zone or with intent to cause harm or panic to persons in a school building or at a school function.

(A) No person, without privilege to do so, shall knowingly do any of the following:

175

(1) Discharge a firearm at or into an occupied structure that is a permanent or temporary habitation of any individual;

(2) Discharge a firearm at, in, or into a school safety zone;

(3) Discharge a firearm within one thousand feet of any school building or of the boundaries of any school premises, with the intent to do any of the following:

(a) Cause physical harm to another who is in the school, in the school building, or at a function or activity associated with the school;

(b) Cause panic or fear of physical harm to another who is in the school, in the school building, or at a function or activity associated with the school;

(c) Cause the evacuation of the school, the school building, or a function or activity associated with the school.

(B) This section does not apply to any officer, agent, or employee of this or any other state or the United States, or to any law enforcement officer, who discharges the firearm while acting within the scope of the officer's, agent's, or employee's duties.

(C) Whoever violates this section is guilty of improperly discharging a firearm at or into a habitation, in a school safety zone, or with the intent to cause harm or panic to persons in a school, in a school building, or at a school function or the evacuation of a school function, a felony of the second degree.

(D) As used in this section, "occupied structure" has the same meaning as in section 2909.01 of the Revised Code.

2923.162 Discharge of firearm on or near prohibited premises.

(A) No person shall do any of the following:

(1) Without permission from the proper officials and subject to division (B)(1) of this section, discharge a firearm upon or over a cemetery or within one hundred yards of a cemetery;

(2) Subject to division (B)(2) of this section, discharge a firearm on a lawn, park, pleasure ground, orchard, or other ground appurtenant to a schoolhouse, church, or inhabited dwelling, the property of another, or a charitable institution;

(3) Discharge a firearm upon or over a public road or highway.

(B)(1) Division (A)(1) of this section does not apply to a person who, while on the person's own land, discharges a firearm.

(2) Division (A)(2) of this section does not apply to a person who owns any type of property described in that division and who, while on the person's own enclosure, discharges a firearm.

(C) Whoever violates this section is guilty of discharge of a firearm on or near prohibited premises. A violation of division (A)(1) or (2) of this section is a misdemeanor of the fourth degree. A violation of division (A)(3) of this section shall be punished as follows:

(1) Except as otherwise provided in division (C)(2), (3), or (4) of this section, a violation of division (A)(3) of this section is a misdemeanor of the first degree.

(2) Except as otherwise provided in division (C)(3) or (4) of this section, if the violation created a substantial risk of physical harm to any person or caused serious physical harm to property, a violation of division (A)(3) of this section is a felony of the third degree.

(3) Except as otherwise provided in division (C)(4) of this section, if the violation caused physical harm to any person, a violation of division (A)(3) of this section is a felony of the second degree.

(4) If the violation caused serious physical harm to any person, a violation of division (A)(3) of this section is a felony of the first degree.

2923.163 Surrender of firearm to law enforcement officer.

If a law enforcement officer stops a person for any law enforcement purpose and the person voluntarily or pursuant to a request or demand of the officer surrenders a firearm to the officer, if a law enforcement officer stops a motor vehicle for any purpose and a person in the motor vehicle voluntarily or pursuant to a request or demand of the officer surrenders a firearm to the officer, or if a law enforcement officer otherwise seizes a firearm from a person, all of the following apply:

(A) If the law enforcement officer does not return the firearm to the person at the termination of the stop or otherwise promptly return the firearm to the person after the seizure of the firearm, the officer or other personnel at the officer's law enforcement agency shall maintain the integrity and identity of the firearm in such a manner so that if the firearm subsequently is to be returned to the person it can be identified and returned to the person in the same condition it was in when it was seized.

(B) If the law enforcement officer does not return the firearm to the person at the termination of the stop or otherwise promptly return the firearm to the person after the seizure of the firearm, if a court finds that a law enforcement officer failed to return the firearm to the person after the person has demanded the return of the firearm from the officer, and if the court orders a law enforcement officer to return the firearm to the person, in addition to any other relief ordered, the court also shall award reasonable costs and attorney's fees to the person who sought the order to return the firearm.

2923.20 Unlawful transaction in weapons.

(A) No person shall:

(1) Recklessly sell, lend, give, or furnish any firearm to any person prohibited by section 2923.13 or 2923.15 of the Revised Code from acquiring or using any firearm, or recklessly sell, lend, give, or furnish any dangerous ordnance to any person prohibited by section 2923.13, 2923.15, or 2923.17 of the Revised Code from acquiring or using any dangerous ordnance;

(2) Possess any firearm or dangerous ordnance with purpose to dispose of it in violation of division (A) of this section;

(3) Manufacture, possess for sale, sell, or furnish to any person other than a law enforcement agency for authorized use in police work, any brass knuckles, cestus, billy, blackjack, sandbag, switchblade knife, springblade knife, gravity knife, or similar weapon;

(4) When transferring any dangerous ordnance to another, negligently fail to require the transferee to exhibit such identification, license, or permit showing him to be authorized to acquire dangerous ordnance pursuant to section 2923.17 of the Revised Code, or negligently fail to take a complete record of the transaction and forthwith forward a copy of that record to the sheriff of the county or safety director or police chief of the municipality where the transaction takes place;

(5) Knowingly fail to report to law enforcement authorities forthwith the loss or theft of any firearm or dangerous ordnance in the person's possession or under the person's control.

(B) Whoever violates this section is guilty of unlawful transactions in weapons. A violation of division (A)(1) or (2) of this section is a felony of the fourth degree. A violation of division (A)(3) or (4) of this section is a misdemeanor of the second degree. A violation of division (A)(5) of this section is a misdemeanor of the fourth degree.

2923.21 Improperly furnishing firearms to minor.

(A) No person shall do any of the following:

(1) Sell any firearm to a person who is under eighteen years of age;

(2) Subject to division (B) of this section, sell any handgun to a person who is under twenty-one years of age;

(3) Furnish any firearm to a person who is under eighteen years of age or, subject to division (B) of this section, furnish any handgun to a person who is under twenty-one years of age, except for lawful hunting, sporting, or educational purposes, including, but not limited to, instruction in firearms or handgun safety, care,

handling, or marksmanship under the supervision or control of a responsible adult;

(4) Sell or furnish a firearm to a person who is eighteen years of age or older if the seller or furnisher knows, or has reason to know, that the person is purchasing or receiving the firearm for the purpose of selling the firearm in violation of division (A)(1) of this section to a person who is under eighteen years of age or for the purpose of furnishing the firearm in violation of division (A)(3) of this section to a person who is under eighteen years of age;

(5) Sell or furnish a handgun to a person who is twenty-one years of age or older if the seller or furnisher knows, or has reason to know, that the person is purchasing or receiving the handgun for the purpose of selling the handgun in violation of division (A)(2) of this section to a person who is under twenty-one years of age or for the purpose of furnishing the handgun in violation of division (A)(3) of this section to a person who is under twenty-one years of age;

(6) Purchase or attempt to purchase any firearm with the intent to sell the firearm in violation of division (A)(1) of this section to a person who is under eighteen years of age or with the intent to furnish the firearm in violation of division (A)(3) of this section to a person who is under eighteen years of age;

(7) Purchase or attempt to purchase any handgun with the intent to sell the handgun in violation of division (A)(2) of this section to a person who is under twenty-one years of age or with the intent to furnish the handgun in violation of division (A)(3) of this section to a person who is under twenty-one years of age.

(B) Divisions (A)(1) and (2) of this section do not apply to the sale or furnishing of a handgun to a person eighteen years of age or older and under twenty-one years of age if the person eighteen years of age or older and under twenty-one years of age is a law enforcement officer who is properly appointed or employed as a law enforcement officer and has received firearms training approved by the Ohio peace officer training council or equivalent firearms training.

(C) Whoever violates this section is guilty of improperly furnishing firearms to a minor, a felony of the fifth degree.

2953.32 Sealing of conviction record or bail forfeiture record.

(A)(1) Except as provided in section 2953.61 of the Revised Code, an eligible offender may apply to the sentencing court if convicted in this state, or to a court of common pleas if convicted in another state or in a federal court, for the sealing of the record of the case that pertains to the conviction. Application may be made at the expiration of three years after the offender's final discharge if convicted of a felony, or at the expiration of one year after the offender's final discharge if convicted of a misdemeanor.

(2) Any person who has been arrested for any misdemeanor offense and who has effected a bail forfeiture for the offense charged may apply to the court in which the misdemeanor criminal case was pending when bail was forfeited for the sealing of the record of the case that pertains to the charge. Except as provided in section 2953.61 of the Revised Code, the application may be filed at any time after the expiration of one year from the date on which the bail forfeiture was entered upon the minutes of the court or the journal, whichever entry occurs first.

(B) Upon the filing of an application under this section, the court shall set a date for a hearing and shall notify the prosecutor for the case of the hearing on the application. The prosecutor may object to the granting of the application by filing an objection with the court prior to the date set for the hearing. The prosecutor shall specify in the objection the reasons for believing a denial of the application is justified. The court shall direct its regular probation officer, a state probation officer, or the department of probation of the county in which the applicant resides to make inquiries and written reports as the court requires concerning the applicant. If the applicant was convicted of or pleaded guilty to a violation of division (A)(2) or (B) of section 2919.21 of the Revised Code, the probation officer or county department of probation that the court directed to make inquiries concerning the applicant shall contact the child support enforcement agency enforcing the applicant's obligations under the child support order to inquire about the offender's compliance with the child support order.

(C)(1) The court shall do each of the following:

(a) Determine whether the applicant is an eligible offender or whether the forfeiture of bail was agreed to by the applicant and the prosecutor in the case. If the applicant applies as an eligible offender pursuant to division (A)(1) of this section and has two or three convictions that result from the same indictment, information, or complaint, from the same plea of guilty, or from the same official proceeding, and result from related criminal acts that were committed within a three-month period but do not result from the same act or from offenses committed at the same time, in making its determination under this division, the court initially shall determine whether it is not in the public interest for the two or three convictions to be counted as one conviction. If the court determines that it is not in the public interest for the two or three convictions to be counted as one conviction, the court shall determine that the applicant is not an eligible offender; if the court does not make that determination, the court shall determine that the offender is an eligible offender.

(b) Determine whether criminal proceedings are pending against the applicant;

(c) If the applicant is an eligible offender who applies pursuant to division (A)(1) of this section, determine whether the applicant has been rehabilitated to the satisfaction of the court;

(d) If the prosecutor has filed an objection in accordance with division (B) of this section, consider the reasons against granting the application specified by the prosecutor in the objection;

(e) Weigh the interests of the applicant in having the records pertaining to the applicant's conviction or bail forfeiture sealed against the legitimate needs, if any, of the government to maintain those records.

(2) If the court determines, after complying with division (C)(1) of this section, that the applicant is an eligible offender or the subject of a bail forfeiture, that no criminal proceeding is pending against the applicant, and that the interests of the applicant in having the records pertaining to the applicant's conviction or bail forfeiture sealed are not outweighed by any legitimate governmental needs to maintain those records, and that the rehabilitation of an applicant who is an eligible offender applying pursuant to division (A)(1) of this section has been attained to the satisfaction of the court, the court, except as provided in divisions (G), (H), or (I) of this section, shall order all official records of the case that pertain to the conviction or bail forfeiture sealed and, except as provided in division (F) of this section, all index references to the case that pertain to the conviction or bail forfeiture deleted and, in the case of bail forfeitures, shall dismiss the charges in the case. The proceedings in the case that pertain to the conviction or bail forfeiture shall be considered not to have occurred and the conviction or bail forfeiture of the person who is the subject of the proceedings shall be sealed, except that upon conviction of a subsequent offense, the sealed record of prior conviction or bail forfeiture may be considered by the court in determining the sentence or other appropriate disposition, including the relief provided for in sections 2953.31 to 2953.33 of the Revised Code.

(3) An applicant may request the sealing of the records of more than one case in a single application under this section. Upon the filing of an application under this section, the applicant, unless indigent, shall pay a fee of fifty dollars, regardless of the number of records the application requests to have sealed. The court shall pay thirty dollars of the fee into the state treasury. It shall pay twenty dollars of the fee into the county general revenue fund if the sealed conviction or bail forfeiture was pursuant to a state statute, or into the general revenue fund of the municipal corporation involved if the sealed conviction or bail forfeiture was pursuant to a municipal ordinance.

(D) Inspection of the sealed records included in the order may be made only by the following persons or for the following purposes:

(1) By a law enforcement officer or prosecutor, or the assistants of either, to determine whether the nature and character of the offense with which a person is to be charged would be affected by virtue of the person's previously having been convicted of a crime;

(2) By the parole or probation officer of the person who is the subject of the records, for the exclusive use of the officer in supervising the person while on parole or under a community control sanction or a post-release control sanction, and in making inquiries and written reports as requested by the court or adult parole authority;

(3) Upon application by the person who is the subject of the records, by the persons named in the application;

(4) By a law enforcement officer who was involved in the case, for use in the officer's defense of a civil action arising out of the officer's involvement in that case;

(5) By a prosecuting attorney or the prosecuting attorney's assistants, to determine a defendant's eligibility to enter a pre-trial diversion program established pursuant to section 2935.36 of the Revised Code;

(6) By any law enforcement agency or any authorized employee of a law enforcement agency or by the department of rehabilitation and correction as part of a background investigation of a person who applies for employment with the agency as a law enforcement officer or with the department as a corrections officer;

(7) By any law enforcement agency or any authorized employee of a law enforcement agency, for the purposes set forth in, and in the manner provided in, section 2953.321 of the Revised Code;

(8) By the bureau of criminal identification and investigation or any authorized employee of the bureau for the purpose of providing information to a board or person pursuant to division (F) or (G) of section 109.57 of the Revised Code;

(9) By the bureau of criminal identification and investigation or any authorized employee of the bureau for the purpose of performing a

criminal history records check on a person to whom a certificate as prescribed in section 109.77 of the Revised Code is to be awarded;

(10) By the bureau of criminal identification and investigation or any authorized employee of the bureau for the purpose of conducting a criminal records check of an individual pursuant to division (B) of section 109.572 of the Revised Code that was requested pursuant to any of the sections identified in division (B)(1) of that section;

(11) By the bureau of criminal identification and investigation, an authorized employee of the bureau, a sheriff, or an authorized employee of a sheriff in connection with a criminal records check described in section 311.41 of the Revised Code;

(12) By the attorney general or an authorized employee of the attorney general or a court for purposes of determining a person's classification pursuant to Chapter 2950. of the Revised Code;

(13) By a court, the registrar of motor vehicles, a prosecuting attorney or the prosecuting attorney's assistants, or a law enforcement officer for the purpose of assessing points against a person under section 4510.036 of the Revised Code or for taking action with regard to points assessed.

When the nature and character of the offense with which a person is to be charged would be affected by the information, it may be used for the purpose of charging the person with an offense.

(E) In any criminal proceeding, proof of any otherwise admissible prior conviction may be introduced and proved, notwithstanding the fact that for any such prior conviction an order of sealing previously was issued pursuant to sections 2953.31 to 2953.36 of the Revised Code.

(F) The person or governmental agency, office, or department that maintains sealed records pertaining to convictions or bail forfeitures that have been sealed pursuant to this section may maintain a manual or computerized index to the sealed records. The index shall contain only the name of, and alphanumeric identifiers that relate to, the persons who are the subject of the sealed records, the word "sealed," and the name of the person, agency, office, or department that has custody of the sealed records, and shall not contain the name of the crime committed. The index shall be made available by the person who has custody of the sealed records only for the purposes set forth in divisions (C), (D), and (E) of this section.

(G) Notwithstanding any provision of this section or section 2953.33 of the Revised Code that requires otherwise, a board of education of a city, local, exempted village, or joint vocational school district that maintains records of an individual who has been permanently excluded under sections 3301.121 and 3313.662 of the Revised Code is permitted to maintain records regarding a conviction that was used as the basis for the individual's permanent exclusion, regardless of a court order to seal the record. An order issued under this section to seal the record of a conviction does not revoke the adjudication order of the superintendent of public instruction to permanently exclude the individual who is the subject of the sealing order. An order issued under this section to seal the record of a conviction of an individual may be presented to a district superintendent as evidence to support the contention that the superintendent should recommend that the permanent exclusion of the individual who is the subject of the sealing order be revoked. Except as otherwise authorized by this division and sections 3301.121 and 3313.662 of the Revised Code, any school employee in possession of or having access to the sealed conviction records of an individual that were the basis of a permanent exclusion of the individual is subject to section 2953.35 of the Revised Code.

(H) For purposes of sections 2953.31 to 2953.36 of the Revised Code, DNA records collected in the DNA database and fingerprints filed for record by the superintendent of the bureau of criminal identification and investigation shall not be sealed unless the superintendent receives a certified copy of a final court order establishing that the offender's conviction has been overturned. For purposes of this section, a court order is not "final" if time remains for an appeal or application for discretionary review with respect to the order.

(I) The sealing of a record under this section does not affect the assessment of points under section 4510.036 of the Revised Code and does not erase points assessed against a person as a result of the sealed record.

2953.33 Restoration of rights and privileges.

(A) An order issued under section 2953.37 of the Revised Code to expunge the record of a person's conviction or, except as provided in division (G) of section 2953.32 of the Revised Code, an order issued under that section to seal the record of a person's conviction restores the person who is the subject of the order to all rights and privileges not otherwise restored by termination of the sentence or community control sanction or by final release on parole or post-release control.

(B)(1) In any application for employment, license, or other right or privilege, any appearance as a witness, or any other inquiry, except as provided in division (E) of section 2953.32 and in section 3319.292 of the Revised Code and subject to division (B)(2) of this section, a person may be questioned only with respect to convictions not sealed, bail forfeitures not expunged under section 2953.42 of the Revised Code as it existed prior to June 29, 1988, and bail forfeitures not sealed, unless the question bears a direct and substantial relationship to the position for which the person is being considered.

(2) A person may not be questioned in any application, appearance, or inquiry of a type described in division (B)(1) of this section with respect to any conviction expunged under section 2953.37 of the Revised Code.

2953.37 Expungement of certain convictions relating to firearms.

(A) As used in this section:

(1) "Expunge" means to destroy, delete, and erase a record as appropriate for the record's physical or electronic form or characteristic so that the record is permanently irretrievable.

(2) "Official records" has the same meaning as in section 2953.51 of the Revised Code.

(3) "Prosecutor" has the same meaning as in section 2953.31 of the Revised Code.

(4) "Record of conviction" means the record related to a conviction of or plea of guilty to an offense.

(B) Any person who is convicted of, was convicted of, pleads guilty to, or has pleaded guilty to a violation of division (B), (C), or (E) of section 2923.16 of the Revised Code as the division existed prior to September 30, 2011, and who is authorized by division (H)(2)(a) of that section to file an application under this section for the expungement of the conviction record may apply to the sentencing court for the expungement of the record of conviction. The person may file the application at any time on or after September 30, 2011. The application shall do all of the following:

(1) Identify the applicant, the offense for which the expungement is sought, the date of the conviction of or plea of guilty to that offense, and the court in which the conviction occurred or the plea of guilty was entered;

(2) Include evidence that the offense was a violation of division (B), (C), or (E) of section 2923.16 of the Revised Code as the division existed prior to September 30, 2011, and that the applicant is authorized by division (H)(2)(a) of that section to file an application under this section;

(3) Include a request for expungement of the record of conviction of that offense under this section.

(C) Upon the filing of an application under division (B) of this section and the payment of the fee described in division (D)(3) of this section if applicable, the court shall set a date for a hearing and shall notify the prosecutor for the case of the hearing on the application. The prosecutor may object to the granting of the application by filing an objection with the court prior to the date set for the hearing. The prosecutor shall specify in the objection the reasons for believing a denial of the application is justified. The court shall direct its regular probation officer, a state probation officer, or the department of probation of the county in which the applicant resides to make inquiries and written reports as the court requires concerning the applicant. The court shall hold the hearing scheduled under this division.

(D)(1) At the hearing held under division (C) of this section, the court shall do each of the following:

(a) Determine whether the applicant has been convicted of or pleaded guilty to a violation of division (E) of section 2923.16 of the Revised Code as the division existed prior to September 30, 2011, and whether the conduct that was the basis of the violation no longer would be a violation of that division on or after September 30, 2011;

(b) Determine whether the applicant has been convicted of or pleaded guilty to a violation of division (B) or (C) of section 2923.16 of the Revised Code as the division existed prior to September 30, 2011, and whether the conduct that was the basis of the violation no longer would be a violation of that division on or after September 30, 2011, due to the application of division (F)(5) of that section as it exists on and after September 30, 2011;

(c) If the prosecutor has filed an objection in accordance with division (C) of this section, consider the reasons against granting the application specified by the prosecutor in the objection;

(d) Weigh the interests of the applicant in having the records pertaining to the applicant's conviction or guilty plea expunged against the legitimate needs, if any, of the government to maintain those records.

(2)(a) The court may order the expungement of all official records pertaining to the case and the deletion of all index references to the case and, if it does order the expungement, shall send notice of the order to each public office or agency that the court has reason to believe may have an official record pertaining to the case if the court, after complying with division (D)(1) of this section, determines both of the following:

(i) That the applicant has been convicted of or pleaded guilty to a violation of division (E) of section 2923.16 of the Revised Code as it existed prior to September 30, 2011, and the conduct that was the basis of the violation no longer would be a violation of that division on or after September 30, 2011, or that the applicant has been convicted of or pleaded guilty to a violation of division (B) or (C) of section 2923.16 of the Revised Code as the division existed prior to September 30, 2011, and the conduct that was the basis of the violation no longer would be a violation of that division on or after September 30, 2011, due to the application of division (F)(5) of that section as it exists on and after September 30, 2011;

(ii) That the interests of the applicant in having the records pertaining to the applicant's conviction or guilty plea expunged are not outweighed by any legitimate needs of the government to maintain those records.

(b) The proceedings in the case that is the subject of an order issued under division (D)(2)(a) of this section shall be considered not to have occurred and the conviction or guilty plea of the person who is the subject of the proceedings shall be expunged. The record of the conviction shall not be used for any purpose, including, but not limited to, a criminal records check under section 109.572 of the Revised Code or a determination under section 2923.125 or 2923.1212 of the Revised Code of eligibility for a concealed handgun license. The applicant may, and the court shall, reply that no record exists with respect to the applicant upon any inquiry into the matter.

(3) Upon the filing of an application under this section, the applicant, unless indigent, shall pay a fee of fifty dollars. The court shall pay thirty dollars of the fee into the state treasury and shall pay twenty dollars of the fee into the county general revenue fund.

Note: These links were accurate as of press time, but no guarantee is given that they are accurate as of the reading of this book.

www.buckeyefirearms.org - Up to date information on anything impacting firearm rights in Ohio. Includes an alert service and newsletter service for free.

http://www.ohioattorneygeneral.gov/Law-Enforcement/Concealed-Carry - Ohio Attorney General's website on concealed carry issues. Will include updates, reciprocity information etc.

www.handgunlaw.us - An excellent website devoted to firearm laws and issues nationwide. Includes a comprehensive database on all 50 states' laws with regard to concealed carry, reciprocity and recognition databases, and general chat forums. Many of the former packing.org gang is here.

www.nra.org - Main page of the National Rifle Association, with links to all of their various programs and information, including the self-defense insurance coverage discussed.

www.house.state.oh.us - Ohio House of Representatives. Read the actual legislation as it is introduced, and learn how to contact your representative.

www.senate.state.oh.us - Ohio Senate. Read the actual legislation as it is introduced, and learn how to contact your senator.

www.fbylaw.com - Webpage of the author's law firm.

www.ohiogunlawguide.com - Webpage for the latest versions of this book. Also, the author is a Type 01 FFL and uses this website as the point of contact for all gun dealer transactions.

http://www.secondcalldefense.org/ - Webpage for Second Call Defense, an excellent self-defense insurance plan.

If you need to reach the author for legal representation, please use khanson@fbylaw.com (740) 363-1213.